GREAT HOUSES

AND

GARDENS

OF

NEW JERSEY

Great Houses

AND

Gardens

OF

New Jersey

CAROLINE SEEBOHM

PHOTOGRAPHS BY PETER C. COOK

RUTGERS UNIVERSITY PRESS

NEW BRUNSWICK, NEW JERSEY

Text © 2003 by Caroline Seebohm

Photographs © 2003 by Peter C. Cook

Map by Yvonne Skaggs

Frontispiece: In Wister Garden a large flower bed, six feet long and four to five
feet deep, is host to this massed display of summer flowers—delphiniums,
columbines, salvias, lupines, and roses—against the south-facing picket fence.

The publication program of Rutgers University Press is supported by
the Board of Governors of Rutgers, The State University of New Jersey.

Manufactured in Singapore

Library of Congress Cataloging-in-Publication Data

Seebohm, Caroline.

Great houses and gardens of New Jersey / Caroline Seebohm ;
photographs by Peter C. Cook.

p. cm.

Includes bibliographical references and index.

ISBN 0-8135-3331-7 (hardcover : alk. paper)

1. Architecture, Domestic—New Jersey.

2. Gardens—New Jersey. I. Cook, Peter C. II. Title.

NA7235.N5S44 2003

728´.37´09749—dc21

2003000229

British Cataloging-in-Publication information
is available from the British Library.

CONTENTS

PREFACE

New Jersey may be the most underestimated state in the union. It is the butt of comedians' jokes, the scorn of restaurant critics, the symbolic home of organized crime, and the nightmare of drivers traversing its interstate highways to get to somewhere better. A book entitled *Great Houses and Gardens of New Jersey*, therefore, may seem to some a laughable misnomer.

They would be wrong.

The state of New Jersey, originally inhabited by the Lenni Lenape Indians and created "Nova Jersey" by the Duke of York in 1664 (after the island of Jersey in Great Britain), embraces New York to its north and Pennsylvania to its west. Although these powerful political and cultural centers cast their shadow over their neighbor in precolonial times, New Jersey had an idiosyncratic personality that came from its immigrant settlers—Germans, Dutch, Swedes, Irish, Scottish, and English, who brought their own culture to the New World, and who exploited the fertile, stream-filled, and mountainous New Jersey countryside to their own benefit with energy and enthusiasm.

As well as developing its agricultural and manufacturing potential, New Jersey was the only region in colonial times to have two institutions of higher education—in Princeton and New Brunswick. Many Quaker thinkers lived and worked in New Jersey. Thomas Paine wrote, "These are the times that try men's souls" at his home in Newark. More recently,

Walt Whitman created much of his oeuvre in Camden, and William Carlos Williams was a doctor and poet in Rutherford until his death in 1963.

After the American Revolutionary War, the major contributions to the country's decorative arts unquestionably came from New York and Philadelphia, and nobody would argue with Benjamin Franklin's alleged pronouncement that New Jersey was "a barrel tapped at both ends." But by the end of the nineteenth century, New Jersey was finding its voice. While house-owners still regarded French and English furniture, textiles, china, and silver to be the standard against which all others must be judged, the carpentry, ceramics, and glass produced in Newark, Elizabeth, Trenton, and New Brunswick began to be recognized as both utilitarian and elegant. (Perhaps the state's inferiority complex was endemic even then, however. On the bottom of a nineteenth-century glass piece is written, "Jersey Glassworks—near New York.")

While the Gilded Age of the late nineteenth century found its expression in the vast mansions built in Newport, Bar Harbor, Manhattan, on Long Island, and along the Hudson River, New Jersey was less noisily producing some extraordinary architecture of its own—close to New York in Pacific Heights, Newark, and Morristown; in the Philadelphia neighborhoods of Camden, Cherry Hill, and Haddonfield; in the state capital, Trenton; and in the conservative enclaves of Bernardsville, Oldwick, Peapack, and Far Hills. New Jersey was never dominated by one family, like New York's Vanderbilts or Delaware's du Ponts, who prescribed the rules for these enormous building programs. Instead, a pleasing diversity emerged, as the various new millionaires migrated through the state and made their own idiosyncratic choices of architecture and gardens, reflecting the pluralistic culture of which most Americans approve.

While the building of bridges and railways continued to change the face of the Northeastern United States through the late nineteenth century, the New Jersey landscape was being "discovered" by American painters, who not only studied the beauties of the Hudson River and points west, but also were inspired by the relaxed atmosphere of the New Jersey shore and the fishing communities along the state's many rivers. Many painters, among them George Inness and Thomas Manley, found that here they could escape the intense pressure of the New York art world or the competitiveness of the Pennsylvania Academy of Fine Arts, the two centers on the East Coast where many had professional connections. One of America's most famous landscape painters, Thomas Eakins, spent several years in Fairton, New Jersey, during his early career, and he painted many scenes along the Cohansey Creek in the 1870s and 1880s. He also painted the shad fishermen in Gloucester, along with portraits of wildlife, hunters, and water sportsmen, his canvases infused with the delicate, soft light that reminded admirers of the French countryside.

Winslow Homer, called by some America's first Impressionist, spent five years painting scenes of the New Jersey coastline, of which *Long Branch, New Jersey* (1869) may be the most well known. "The atmosphere of the place is sensuous, crass, and earthy," Homer wrote of the New Jersey shore. "Representatives of all classes are to be met: heavy merchants, railroad magnates, distinguished soldiers, editors, musicians, politicians, and divines, and all are on an easy level of temporary equality."

It is this eclecticism that emerges from the pages of this book. A "great" house, for the purposes of the authors, is one that is inimitably of its time and place in this most culturally diverse of states. Thus we examine a prerevolutionary Dutch farmhouse that could have sprung from the coast of Devon in England; a brick-patterned house that vividly expresses the originality and exuberance of the region's early builders and craftsmen; a collection of native stone buildings that are reminiscent of Bucks County, Pennsylvania; and an Arts and Crafts house with contributions by New Jersey's most famous furniture-maker, Gustav Stickley. The twentieth century is equally well represented with works by masters of their period, such as Frank Lloyd Wright, Robert Venturi, Michael Graves, and Richard Meier.

A "great" garden also offers a democracy of meaning, ranging from the natural landscapes with native plants, trees, and streams that date back three hundred years and inspired so many early American artists, to the formal French parterres, Japanese rock gardens, and English herbaceous borders that reflect the influence of countless trips abroad over the last two centuries. That New Jersey is called the "Garden State" is attributed mostly to its sumptuous tomato and corn harvests, but the astonishing beauty and diversity of its flower and woodland gardens prove the justice of its all-encompassing denomination.

The only editorial criteria for inclusion in the book were that the house and/or garden had to be privately owned and not open to the public. Thus some houses that undoubtedly deserve the adjective "great," such as Skylands in Ringwood State Park, the Ballantine House in Newark, Lambert Castle in Paterson, the Schuyler-Hamilton House, the Ford Mansion, and the Wick House in Morristown, Morven in Princeton, the Thomas Revell House in Burlington, the Israel Crane House in Montclair, Georgian Court in Lakewood, Craftsman Farms in Parsippany, the Emlen Physick House in Cape May, and Pomona Hall in Camden, did not make the cut. For the same reason, we also had to exclude the James Rose Garden in Ridgewood, the Van Vleck House and Gardens in Montclair, the Reeves-Reed Arboretum in Summit, and the Doris Duke Gardens in Somerville. We admit, however, to bending the rules on occasion when historical or aesthetic arguments prevailed, so a few houses and gardens represented here are open by appointment according to local Garden Club or other organizations' ordinances.

There are, of course, countless wonderful houses and gardens in New Jersey that remain unrecognized here. One book cannot do justice to them all. Indeed, the plethora of fine architecture and landscape design revealed in these pages may surprise those who think of New Jersey as only a traffic-clogged artery running through the Northeast corridor between New York and Washington. While artists have long known its secret, we believe that this book will reveal to many others some of the unsung glories of the Garden State.

ACKNOWLEDGMENTS

First and foremost, we should like to thank the owners of the houses and gardens that appear in this book. Without them, there would be no book. We are most grateful for their generosity, patience, and hospitality.

We should also like to thank the following for their help in providing ideas, contacts, and other sustenance during the making of this book: Ken Druse, Barbara Grogan, Richard Herpster, Rosemary Johnson, Leeann Lavin, Ronald E. Magill, David Major, John McPhee, Kathy Mellon, Barbara Paca, Anne Reeves, Paula Sculley, Shelley Sutton, and Barry Thomson. For unstinting help and suggestions, we wish to thank most especially Pat Ryan at Turpin Real Estate in Far Hills, Annabelle Radcliffe-Trenner and Michael Calafati at Historic Building Architects in Trenton, Ulysses Dietz at the Newark Museum, and Arlene Minder at The Greenhouse in Deal.

Special thanks go to Howard Siskowitz for his icon in the authors' photograph (with apologies to Grant Wood's *American Gothic*), Richard Speedy, Richard Speedy Studio, Hopewell, New Jersey, and to Taylor Photo, Princeton, New Jersey.

Finally, the book would not exist without the admirable support of the Rutgers University Press team who worked with us: our editor, Leslie Mitchner, Melanie Halkias, Molly Baab, and Alison Hack.

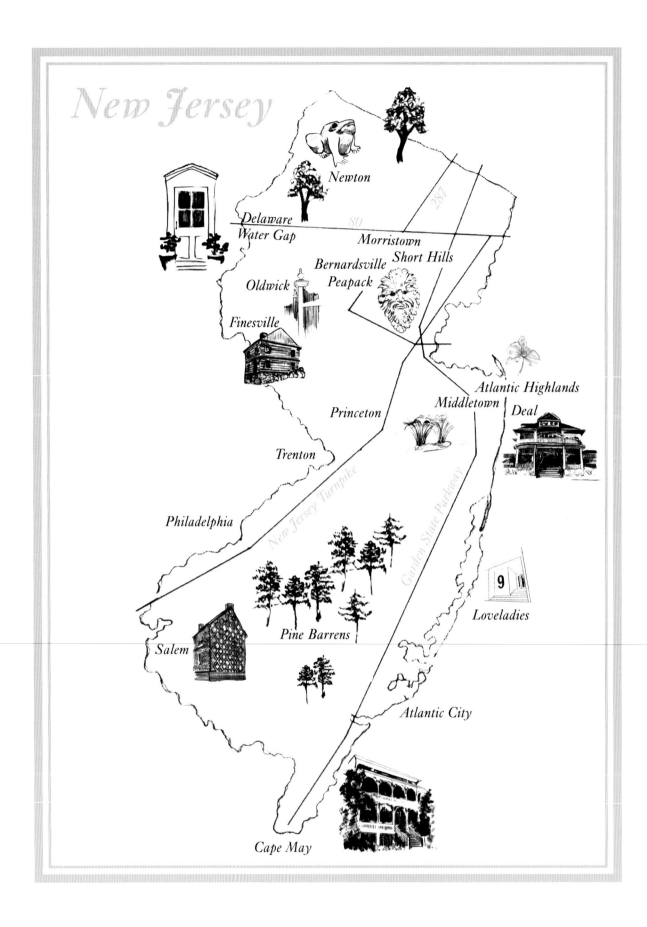

New Jersey

Newton

Delaware
Water Gap

Morristown

Bernardsville   Short Hills
Peapack

Oldwick

Finesville

Atlantic Highlands

Middletown   Deal

Princeton

Trenton

Philadelphia

9

Loveladies

Pine Barrens

Salem

Atlantic City

Cape May

GREAT HOUSES

AND

GARDENS

OF

NEW JERSEY

Allen and Hella Lacy Garden

LINWOOD, ATLANTIC COUNTY

It is always interesting to see how professionals in the art of living decide to live themselves. What kind of architecture do architects choose for their homes? What forms of art do artists surround themselves with? Allen Lacy is a distinguished garden writer and teacher whose books on gardening are greatly valued. He was a regular garden columnist for the *New York Times* and the *Wall Street Journal* for many years, and then in 1983 he began publishing a newsletter, *Homeground*, which continues to provide a source of pleasure and information to garden-lovers. His most recent book is *A Year in Our Gardens: Letters of Nancy Goodwin and Allen Lacy*, published in 2001 by the University of North Carolina Press.

As well as feeding his gardening passion, since moving to New Jersey in 1970, he has always had another day job—as a professor of philosophy for some thirty years at the Richard Stockton College of New Jersey, from which he retired in 1999. These dual passions, of "dahlias and Descartes," as he puts it, make for a stimulating combination. He expresses gratitude to his students "who have borne with me when, in the midst of a discussion of Plato's *Republic*, I have suddenly launched into a description of a flower-seed farm in Costa Rica founded by Claude Hope, a horticultural equivalent of Plato's philosopher-king."

With these dazzling credentials, one might anticipate that his own garden would reflect the encyclopedic scale of his horticultural knowledge and expertise. Indeed, in a way it does. But in other, more profound ways, it is an agreeable surprise, because, instead of being Allen

FACING *Past the front of the house, a small path takes the visitor under a rustic wrought-iron archway into a wild cottage garden, with perennials such as bleeding hearts, daylilies, Japanese anemones, and lots of bulbs in the spring.*

Lacy's sole creation, it is a cocreation reflecting the aesthetic vision of his wife and life's companion, Hella.

Hella and Allen Lacy's garden occupies a lot comprising only 100 by 155 feet on a busy road in the middle of the small southeastern New Jersey town of Linwood, not far from Atlantic City. The house, originally a farmhouse built around 1812, is one of the oldest houses in town. Small and covered with gray siding, it sits in the center of the modest property, offering little exterior drama. When the Lacys bought it in 1971 and moved in with their two sons, Paul and Michael, there was no garden to speak of, except for a few juniper trees and that ubiquitous garden prop of American landscape design, a dreary carpet of lawn. The

ABOVE LEFT *In an*
island carved out of the back
deck, containers are buried
in the ground, exploding with
cannas, ginger lilies, plumbago,
brugmansia, and pennisetum
in a mini-forest of color.

ABOVE RIGHT *An elaborate*
display of container plants—
lantana, coleus, plumbago, and
pennisetum—forms a dazzling
invitation to the modest front
entrance of the house.

house and yard were open to the street, so passing cars could grab a view of the exposed inhabitants—and vice versa.

Today, it is unrecognizable. That unassuming, uninteresting plot has been transformed
into a tiny jungle, a protected sanctuary of herbaceous perennials and annuals, shrubs, and
small trees, all awash in color, scent, and sensuousness. The impact is achieved largely by its
signature feature—a massed array of containers (179 so far) grouped and planted in the most
striking and original fashion.

To create this small paradise, the Lacys had to embark on a formidable series of structural alterations and additions, carried over a protracted period of years. Along one side of
the house and part of its back, they built, at different levels, three interlocking decks to provide walkways, places to sit, and platforms for their constantly enlarging collection of containers. They installed French doors opening out from the living room to their largest deck
and added a pergola for shade and for hanging plants. In the front of the house, they created
a wild cottage garden entered through a wrought-iron arch, inviting the visitor to enjoy an
experience reminiscent of the English countryside.

In what Allen Lacy calls "the dirt part of our garden," the part that is not occupied by
decks, the Lacys planted trees—quince, dogwood, holly, and dawn redwood. They also put
in shrubs—bayberry, winter jasmine, clove currant, abelia, and deutzias. Out front, they
planted a one-gallon pot of yellow-groove bamboo, which eventually became a large grove
serving as a backdrop to their cottage garden and providing privacy from the busy street.

Under the trees that separate the house from its neighbors, a dense planting of deutzia, hostas, and colorful caladiums promotes privacy.

They endowed their piece of suburban real estate with perennials, such as bleeding hearts, Japanese anemones, daylilies, thalictrum, hellebores, and over fifty cultivars of hosta. They planted bulbs—hundreds of daffodils, along with snowdrops, Grecian anemones, special tulips, and grape hyacinths. They festooned their pergola with a hardy kiwi vine that must be pruned four times a year and provides a large crop of tart, but tasty, small green fruits every October. They carved out an island in the center of the back deck, where brightly colored plants, such as cannas, ginger lilies, and brugmansias, now rise up to astonishing heights like sailing ships at anchor in the silver-gray ocean of the surrounding deck.

One of the gorgeous specimens that the Lacys cultivate in their greenhouse—Datura metel 'Cornucopoeia.'

But the key to this garden is the containers, all 179 of them. (Inside the house there are another 50 containers, mostly hanging baskets, all tended exclusively by Hella.) Of course many gardening cultures have recognized the potential of containers. The Chinese traditionally use pots in their rock and water gardens, not only for focal points of color as in a painting, but also to give flexibility to the canvas as a whole. The Renaissance English garden depended on pots as well as boxwood for its formal effects. When Longleat House, the great English stately home in Wiltshire, was built in 1572, 3,000 containers were ordered for the main terrace. Allen and Hella Lacy's garden is somewhat smaller than Longleat, but the impact is similar. Every year they fill their urns, barrels, and baskets with different mixtures of flowering annuals, along with architectural, colorful, and intriguing plants, such as cannas ('Australia,' 'Panache,' and 'Pretoria'), tropical hibiscus, passion flowers, and pentas. Special attention is paid to foliage plants like *Altermanthera rubiginosa* 'Dentata,' caladiums, and elephant ears, including 'Black Magic,' which is stunning for its large, matte-like leaves. The Lacys are especially fond of coleus, managing to keep over thirty cultivars going from one year to the next by overwintering cuttings in their greenhouse.

According to the Lacys, container gardening offers a wonderful combination of control and flexibility. There are no weeds to contend with. Plant diseases and insect infestations are spotted quickly and dealt with. Many distinctive plants can be harmoniously combined in one container, as long as they all have the same cultural requirements. If color clashes turn up, they can be corrected quickly and easily by moving one container or the other. And, thanks to the greenhouse, the Lacy garden is a twelve-month affair. When cold weather arrives, many of their containers simply move a few feet, from deck to greenhouse.

For a small garden, the design is complex, and complexity demands hard work. Allen Lacy shirks some chores. He has reduced his lawn to a tiny patch that can be mowed in seven minutes and has never been rolled. He has never double-dug a flower bed or tested his soil. "And finally," he confesses, "I have never committed topiary, and don't plan to." But there is one duty that he attends to assiduously. The soil is mostly sand, which requires constant watering. An irrigation system takes care of the "dirt parts" of the garden, but their containers must be watered by hand, daily, and sometimes twice a day if it's especially hot and windy. Both Lacys spend hours every day in summer weather, holding a hose.

The Lacy household is cosmopolitan, in that Hella grew up in Germany during World War II, and Allen grew up in Texas, where his mother grew jasmine in pots outside the house, mixed with red hibiscus and blue Cape plumbago. As a Texan transplanted to New Jersey via South Carolina, Virginia, Michigan, and upstate New York, Allen has a keen understanding of geography, exemplified by what he wrote in one of his newsletters:

> Our garden would be impoverished without its host of plants from the far corners of the world, courtesy of a host of plant explorers. Early Spanish missionaries to South America brought back nasturtiums from Argentina and four o'clocks from Peru. For begonias and fuchsias we must be grateful for Father Charles Plumier (for whom the genus *Plumeria* is named) who discovered them in Santo Domingo. Alexander von Humboldt and Aime Bonpland gave us scarlet sage from Mexico and the Victoria water lily from Bolivia. To John and William Bartram, the eighteenth-century Philadelphia Quaker botanists, we are indebted for rescuing *Franklinia alatamaha*, on the very eve of its extinction in the wilds of Georgia. (*Homeground*, Summer 1997)

"Gardening engages the mind in an unending quest for knowledge," Allen Lacy observes, "for it would take many lifetimes to know and understand everything in even one small garden like ours." He notes that the pleasures of gardening take three forms. There are the sensual pleasures of sight, touch, and smell. There are the pleasures of the intellect. Finally and most importantly, there are the spiritual rewards that gardens offer—the sense of stewardship and caring for living things, the friendships that spring up among those who garden, and the special companionship of people like the Lacys, who have shared a life and devoted so much of it to the raising of their two sons and to the making of their garden.

Frick Garden

ALPINE, BERGEN COUNTY

Bergen County received its first legal charter in 1683, then a much larger county than it is now. Its claim to significance lies largely in its position along the Hudson River, with the high cliffs of the Palisades creating a dramatic panorama for those looking for congenial surroundings within easy reach of New York City. With the disappearance of the Lenni Lenape Indians, as in most of New Jersey, European settlers built farms and residences in areas that are now part of Palisades Interstate Park. Several old houses have been preserved here, including the Blackledge-Kearny House in Alpine, once believed to be the headquarters of the English general Lord Cornwallis during the hostilities along the Hudson River with George Washington at the time of the Revolutionary War.

By the end of the nineteenth century, Alpine had grown into a very prosperous suburb, home to the famous architects Calvert Vaux (1824–1895) and J. Cleveland Cady (1837–1919). The latter designed the stone community church, distinctive for its High Gothic architecture. While impressive houses and gardens sprang up in answer to the great Gilded Age mansions of Somerset and Hunterdon Counties, many were demolished or rebuilt during the difficult economic times that afflicted much of the twentieth century. New houses now dominate the landscape, but few have the delightful garden landscape that defines Dr. and Mrs. Henry Clay Frick's estate not far from the Palisades.

FACING *A barn transported from a local farm became the starting point of a walled garden. The exuberant rose bushes are kept in check by clipped boxwood in squares and circles reminiscent of seventeenth-century French and English parterre gardens.*

9

The Palladian-style architecture of the house dates from the 1940s, offering a creamy backdrop for the hundreds of pale pink and white 'New Dawn,' 'City of York,' and 'Blair #2' roses that cascade down the stone walls of the patio.

The loggia is garlanded with roses, copied from the gardens of Old Westbury on Long Island. The powerful blue of the agapanthus flowers creates a striking contrast of color.

The house was built in the mid-1940s, but when the Fricks married twenty-one years ago, Emily Frick decided that the architecture of the house needed some changes, and she brought in an architect who created a more classical feel, with Palladian windows and arches. "It was experimental," she says, "but I was interested in classical architecture, and so we adapted the house to that style."

As for the garden, the changes were far more radical. The house sat on approximately sixty acres of steeply graded land, with a pond at the far end, and some fine specimen trees that had been brought in during the 1950s from the Frick family pinetum on Long Island. Mrs. Frick, a keen gardener, started modestly with a small, walled garden at the back of the house behind a barn, which had been transported there from a neighboring farm when the house was first built. Gradually the garden landscape expanded as Mrs. Frick continued to

ABOVE *The woodland garden meanders down a gentle slope through trees and along a natural stream towards a pond where two weeping cherries strike a pose. The rocks are dotted with shade plants—iris, primrose, hosta, and wild orchids.*

RIGHT *An impressive stand of auriculas and ferns makes this part of the woodland garden both colorful and highly textured.*

ABOVE *Thousands of bluebells planted over fifteen years ago bloom in late spring, transforming the woodland floor into a sea of color as far as the eye can see.*

RIGHT *A row of glamorous yellow Japanese tree peonies blooms in front of a trellised entryway to the swimming pool, another idea brought back from a garden in England.*

experiment, using her knowledge acquired by countless visits to European gardens the couple visited over the years—especially in England.

She filled the walled garden with old-fashioned roses, including 'New Dawn,' 'Zephyrine Drouhin,' and 'Blair #2,' contained in a framework of boxwood, like the eighteenth-century parterre gardens she had seen in England and France. She planted a multitude of 'New Dawn,' 'City of York,' and 'Blair #2' roses along the loggia of the house and trained them over the arches, thus creating a series of garlands that she copied from the Old Westbury Gardens on Long Island. She designed a trellised pergola at the entrance to the swimming pool, another idea from abroad. She is completely relaxed about copying design schemes from other gardens. "A picture is worth a thousand words in the continual challenge of communication between the creators and their disciples," she says cheerfully. Indeed, she is following a strong tradition of gardeners' plagiarism. How many laburnum walks have been

The steps leading to the patio at the back of the house are decorated with a very ornate wrought-iron railing and a profusion of plants in containers—orchids, geraniums, and agapanthus.

replicated in the United States from the famous one created by the late Rosemary Verey at Barnsley House in Gloucestershire, England?

A few years ago, Dr. Frick became unwell, and his wife decided to create a woodland garden with him—"something we could do together," she said. They started planting water and shade plants along a natural stream originating from the Palisades that trickles down a small hillside to the pond at the far end of the property. Rocks and large-leaved plants create a theatrical background for the delicate irises, native ginger, primroses, hostas, wild orchids, auriculas, and other plants that bring grace and color to this water garden. To the left of the stream is a wood, underplanted with thousands of bluebells, another labor of love started over fifteen years ago.

But Mrs. Frick not only is a gardener of great creativity. She also harbors a passion that is the mark of a true devotee of the plant kingdom. She has a collection of over 2,500 orchids. The obsession started as a way of filling the two greenhouses that her husband gave her as a birthday present in 1987. The greenhouses are tucked away in a former donkey field at the north end of the property, concealing their treasures most effectively. To those inside these glasshouses, however, the astonishing shapes and colors of hundreds of specimen orchids reveal themselves like rows of fireworks exploding in unison.

The chief minder of these singular blooms is horticulturalist David H. Booth, a former estate manager in England whom the Fricks brought over to America almost twenty years ago. He now spends a large part of his time tending the orchids and roses, along with the masses of potted plants that decorate the terrace and the interior of the house all year round.

The orchids, however, take up most of his energy. David Booth regards his orchids as though they were his babies. They are as fragile as infants and need constant care. He has to repot sixty percent of these plants every year, using over half a ton of compost, a staggering task. Some orchids take eight to ten years to flower. Others refuse to flower at all. Some are so delicate that they need minute-by-minute attention. Orchid-growing is not for the faint-hearted.

Not only does David Booth propagate, nurture, experiment, and constantly find new species by cross-fertilizing with other orchid-growers, but he and Mrs. Frick are also fiercely competitive, entering their best blooms in orchid shows across the country. They have won many awards, including several from the American Orchid Society, and most recently a First-Class Certificate from the Society that is rarely granted. A favorite specimen of both Mrs. Frick and David Booth is the *Multiflora paphiopedilum* 'Rothschildeanum Borneo × Chase E'—a new species, rare, and an Award of Merit prizewinner. Another triumph of propagation, the *Paphiopedilum* 'Prince Edward of York,' has been given the name "Emily," after its owner.

The rewards of growing orchids are obvious. Apart from their subtle range of colors and forms, the blossoms are unlike those of any other flower, some looking as dangerous as jackals, others as innocent as lambs. It's a lifelong fascination, filled with delight, disappointment, and surprise. Perhaps the greatest reward is that from January to April, peak blooming time, the Fricks' house is transformed into a jungle, when these treasured specimens with their exotic names—phalaenopsis, paphiopedilum, calanthe, cymbidium—are let out of their glass cages for their moment of glory.

E. C. Knight House

CAPE MAY, CAPE MAY COUNTY

Cape May is at the southernmost tip of the state of New Jersey, so far down the East Coast, in fact, that it is south of the Mason-Dixon line. It sits at the end of a long spit of land between the Atlantic Ocean and Delaware Bay. Blessed by sea breezes and the soft waters of the bay, it was originally settled, as was so much of New Jersey, by Lenni Lenape Indians. By the mid-seventeenth century white explorers had started their journey along the coast, and, in 1620, so one story goes, Captain Cornelius Jacobsen Mey, a Dutchman, laid claim to this tip of land and named it Cape May after himself. Other historians point to the fact that the area was called Cape Island throughout the early days and well into the nineteenth century, when the local newspaper, the *Cape May Ocean Wave*, was founded, its title a confirmation of the town's official name.

The most significant hint of Cape May's future glory is found in an advertisement that appeared in the *Pennsylvania Gazette* in 1766 announcing for sale a "Valuable Plantation, containing 254 Acres of Land, Marsh and Swamp, Part of the Swamp cleared ... the rest well timbered and watered, with a large good two Story House and Kitchen, a very good Barn and Stable and Garden." The final sentence gives the game away: "Pleasantly situated, open to the Sea, in the Lower Precinct of the County of Cape May, and within One Mile and a Half of the Sea Shore; where a Number resort for Health, and bathing in the Water."

FACING *The second-floor verandah shows Stephen Button's artistry with wood, the balustrades and arches bearing the characteristic style of his architecture.*

19

Stephen Button (1813–1897), the premier architect of nineteenth-century Cape May, completed this house for E. C. Knight in 1881, after a fire had destroyed much of the town. Its ornate woodwork, balustrades, and bracketed arches typify it as an "American Bracketed Villa."

"Resort for Health, and bathing in the Water"—the author of this sales pitch was Robert Parsons, a gentleman who clearly saw the potential of Cape May for those looking for somewhere to escape the summer heat and pollution of the rapidly expanding industrial cities to the north. How right he was! By the early 1800s large numbers of wealthy Philadelphians, along with citizens of other neighboring states, were "discovering" Cape May and building summer houses in what was then still regarded as part of the South, just as Princeton was considered a southern university until the last century. (Mr. Parsons's use of the word "plantation" in his groundbreaking advertisement seems also to reflect this perception, although the word was used sometimes to describe estates in other parts of New Jersey.) By the mid-1800s steamboats were traveling daily from Philadelphia to Cape May, transporting eager tourists for a round-trip fare of six dollars. By the end of the Civil War, trains also made the run from Boston, New York, Philadelphia, and Baltimore.

The visitors who came to Cape May in those days stayed in hotels, which appeared like wildfire to satisfy the demand. For the 1865 season, twenty-two hotels were open for business, one of the most important being Congress Hall. Originally a wood-frame boarding-

Stephen Button was well known for his walk-through windows, two-story verandahs at the front and rear, and elaborate wood-carved brackets and eaves.

house built by Thomas H. Hughes in 1816, by mid-century it had been remodeled into a grand palace, two hundred fifty feet long and forty-two feet wide, with a wing ninety feet long, balconies, gable-roofs, and a huge bathhouse with cabanas on the beach. "At night," as a visitor described it, "when this hall is cleared of tables and chairs, and hundreds of gas jets are brilliantly burning and flickering and the gay of the elite are flushed with the giddy dance, then you behold a ball-scene, beautiful and fair." The other great hotel of the era was the Mount Vernon, described by the *Illustrated London News* of 1853 as "a palatial building far exceeding any hotel in England." The four-story hotel was planned to accommodate 3,500 guests. Before it was finished, a fire destroyed the whole structure in 1856, prefiguring a more catastrophic conflagration that was to cripple Cape May only twenty-two years later.

Although these hotels compared in grandeur to the great hotels Henry Flagler began to build on the eastern coast of Florida, Cape May never succumbed to the notion that its survival as a resort depended solely on these public establishments. Many wealthy Philadelphia summer residents decided they preferred more exclusive private houses and imported their own architects to do the job for them. The so-called "cottage era" in Cape May was spearheaded by a well-known Philadelphia lawyer and developer, John C. Bullitt, and his partner, Frederick Fairthorne, who bought the Columbia House hotel and then subdivided the tract opposite, creating Columbia Avenue and Gurney Street. On these lots were built the first of what became regarded as typical Cape May cottages, and the architect of three of those on Columbia Avenue that still stand, as well as many others in the town, was Stephen Decatur Button.

The sides of the house are less ornate than the front, with plain eaves and shutters, while the ceiling of the verandah displays elegant beam-work.

Stephen Button (1813–1897) was born in Preston, Connecticut. At sixteen he was apprenticed as a carpenter, and five years later he began training as an architect in New York under George Purvis, a Scot who had been with the Cubitt Brothers in London before moving to America. In the 1840s Button gravitated to the South, and, after moving to Montgomery, Alabama, he did some highly regarded work in Columbus, Georgia. During this period of his career, Southern architecture, influenced by European models, reinforced the style he had learned under Purvis and became part of his permanent architectural vocabulary.

Button returned north in 1848 and settled in Philadelphia, starting a practice with his brother-in-law, Joseph C. Hoxie. Button's work was immediately very successful in the Philadelphia area, and it was not surprising that John Bullitt hired him in 1863 for his expansion of the Columbia House in Cape May and for the developments on the adjacent lots. Button produced for his client a series of cottages that were similar in style. Made of wood, they had a center hall, with two rooms on one side and a long parlor running the length of the house on the opposite side. The measurements of all his interiors were mathematically worked out, following classical proportions, so that all of them bear an air of symmetry and simplicity. His

*From an upstairs window, the ocean can plainly be seen. The house is unusually high off
the ground, it is said because E. C. Knight wanted an unobstructed view of the water.*

exteriors were also symmetrical—generally three stories in height, subtly Italianate in feel,
with a pitched roof, two chimneys, and a decorative second floor (or piano nobile) with balconies, double front doors, bays, eaves, balustrades, and columns. One of Button's trade-
marks was the use of cast iron, which was both durable and inexpensive, and his houses were
often greatly enhanced by the addition of elaborate cast-iron ornament.

While Button was making his respectable statements on Columbia Avenue, another architect, Frank Furness, was shocking the neighbors not far away on Washington Street. In
1877 Furness started designing a house for Emlen Physick, the son of a wealthy Philadelphia doctor who bequeathed his fortune to his son on the condition that he follow the family tradition of medicine. The younger Physick seems to have ignored his father's wishes,

instead commissioning Furness to build a large and stylistically complex house in Cape May for his summer pleasure. Furness was a student of Richard Morris Hunt, the darling of New York society, whose grand clients included Alva Belmont. Marble House, her house in Newport, was one of Hunt's masterpieces. Hunt's work could hardly have differed more greatly from that of Stephen Button. Flamboyant, eccentric, using a variety of materials and styles, including the Stick Style and High Gothic, Hunt encouraged his protégé to exhibit a similar enthusiasm for excess, as the Emlen Physick House bears witness, with its flat roof, huge chimneys, heavily ornamented dormers, and carved decoration, reflecting throughout the façade powerful Tudor and Gothic influences.

The Emlen Physick House was almost finished when, in 1878, a huge fire broke out and demolished the center of Cape May. The damage was unimaginable. Seven hotels were reduced to rubble in the blaze, including Congress Hall and the Columbia. Over thirty cottages and boardinghouses were also destroyed. The whole catastrophe took place in less than twenty-four hours. Hand-wringing was the order of the day, and blame was lavished on everyone and everything, from the firefighters who were accused of inefficiency, to the failure of the water supply, evidence of egregious unpreparedness in view of the fact that most of the Cape May buildings were made of wood. The latter was a particularly pitiable revelation since, as the *Philadelphia Evening Bulletin* pointed out, "the Atlantic Ocean was but a stone's throw from the burning buildings."

But with typical American optimism and energy, within a few years Cape May was rising from the ashes. The big question remained—what would the city's post-fire architecture look like? By the late 1880s the giants of American architecture included the Hunt Brothers; McKim, Mead & White; Delano & Aldrich; and Charles Platt, most of whom had been trained in the Beaux-Arts tradition and had branched out into expansive designs based on Jacobean, Gothic, Italianate, Queen Anne, Eastlake, Stick, and other eclectic styles. This was an explosive period for American architecture. Newport, Rhode Island, the new mecca for the wealthy and Cape May's competition to the north, was becoming a showplace for the stunning Victorian and Romanesque mansions designed by Hunt and his colleagues, while even farther north, the huge shingle-style "cottages" pioneered by Boston architects Rotch & Tilden, William Ralph Emerson, and New York's Bruce Price were transforming Bar Harbor, Maine, from a fishing village into the latest summer paradise for the rich.

Cape May, however, in a sturdy rejection of contemporary fashion, turned its back on these radical exercises in Gilded Age exhibitionism and declared its faith in the familiar boxy look of Button's classically proportioned cottages. Part of the reason was practical, as Emil R. Salvini points out in his illustrated history of Cape May, *The Summer City by the Sea*: "Because the majority of cottages built after the fire were constructed without architectural plans, it was common for carpenters to follow the lines of existing cottages or lift designs from the popular pattern books." The result was a startling degree of uniformity. Salvini

*The finials that decorate the cast-iron railings surrounding the house
are finished in the characteristically ornate style of the architect.*

writes, "In the case of Cape May, most were styled after the simply ornamented Italianate 'Button' style that the resort had fallen in love with decades before the fire."

So Stephen Button, who in other parts of the country would have been regarded as hopelessly old-fashioned, remained Cape May's favorite son, and, to the gratitude of posterity, incidentally safeguarded the appealingly specific architectural identity of the town. He designed two big hotels to replace those lost—the Windsor and the Lafayette. The commission for a new Congress Hall—this time made of brick—was given to a little-known architect, J. F. Meyer; Button was called in shortly afterwards to improve it and add a two-thousand-square-foot music pavilion. Button was also commissioned to build two private residences adjacent to each other to the rear of Congress Hall, facing a new post-fire street called Congress Place. One of them is the E. C. Knight House, owned today by Robert Wilson, his wife, Anne Wright Wilson, and their family.

Edward C. Knight, a Philadelphia businessman, was the owner of the Atlantic Hotel, another victim of the fire. He decided not to rebuild it, instead commissioning Stephen Button to develop the land as the Atlantic Terrace cottages. That year Knight commissioned Button to build him a house on the newly formed Congress Place opposite the hotel. (Knight was chairman of the board of Congress Hall and oversaw its resurrection in 1881.) His house, also completed in 1881, is larger than many of Button's designs, with eight bedrooms and a basement with a screened porch. It is said that a deed was drawn up preventing anything being built in front of it because Knight wanted an unobstructed view of the ocean. The house is raised unusually high off the ground, perhaps another technique for securing a good view. The architecture exhibits typical Button design features—walk-through windows, double-front doors, two-story verandahs at the front and rear, overhanging eaves, and a cast-iron "widow's walk" on the roof. Another trademark of Button's work is the elaborate bracket carving (perhaps reflecting his early years as a carpenter), which is well in evidence here. In some architectural texts, the E. C. Knight House is called a typical example of the "American Bracketed Villa."

For a while, Cape May's revival was the talk of the expanding class of industrial millionaires, and fashionable people flocked back to the ocean resort. President Benjamin Harrison spent his summers there in 1890 and 1891, using Congress Hall as his office (originating the idea of a summer White House). John Philip Sousa played every summer on the lawn outside the hotel (hence the "Congress Hall March"). President Garfield's daughter got married there. John Wanamaker of the Philadelphia department store was a regular summer resident, and Main Line Philadelphians continued to enjoy the summer motor races sponsored by Chevrolet and Ford that Cape May, with its unusually wide beaches, could accommodate. House-building went on at a rapid pace, with Button's architecture as the dominating model. As Emil Salvini points out, "Cape May approached the twentieth century with its major hotels and many of its cottages designed or influenced by a man born almost fifty years before the start of the Civil War."

Could this in part have had something to do with its rapid decline as the new century dawned? For by 1910, Cape May had lost its glamour, and all the people who had formerly loved it were now abandoning it. Atlantic City, with its long boardwalk and gambling casinos, suddenly looked much more exciting. Cape May's pretty little houses and small streets did not sit so well with the new, modern generation that was seeking thrills of a more cutting-edge nature and looking for living spaces made of steel and glass, not gingerbread. In a move showing the extent of the town's loss of prestige, even Edward C. Knight left Cape May and moved up north to Newport.

For many years his daughter Anne lived in the house. After 1933, it was owned by four different groups, and in 1970 it was turned into a bed-and-breakfast, like many other Cape May houses built during the 1880s and 1890s. A Pennsylvania corporation owned it in 1991, and at that point the Wilsons stepped in and purchased the property.

The E. C. Knight House is now back in private hands, as it was originally designed for. The Wilsons are well aware of its history (Anne is an architectural design consultant), and they have restored it with great care and respect for the original architecture, much of which was still in place. (They were helped by Princeton architects Holt & Morgan and garden consultant Stan Sperlak of Cape Shore.) The trim is original, but the balustrades are new. "We found the originals in the attic and had them copied," Anne Wright Wilson says.

During this time, like the E. C. Knight House, Cape May itself has had yet another apotheosis, having become today one of the most desirable and popular resorts in the Northeast. Its architecture, once questioned for its uniformity and conventionality, is now treasured as one of the most authentic examples of the Victorian era in America, and most of Cape May's downtown area is a National Historic Landmark (the only town so designated in the whole of the United States).

Raised unusually high off the ground, the house displays a fine border of flowers partially concealing the latticework that protects the lower level.

Perhaps the ultimate testament to Cape May's transformation is the rebirth of Congress Hall, the hotel that went from being the most fabulous stopping-off place for America's rich to a bankrupt, dilapidated pile of brick. It has now been restored to the tune of twenty-five million dollars by Curtis Bashaw, whose grandfather, the late Reverend Carl McIntire, used to hold his Cape May Bible Conference there until about ten years ago. Those eager to discover religious themes in American life may like this accident of history, for the story of Cape May has a redemptive element, in terms of its faith in itself and in its bid for immortality. If one believed in the afterlife, Stephen Decatur Button, whose E. C. Knight House has overlooked Congress Hall throughout its changing fortunes, would surely be smiling.

A Converted Barn

Central New Jersey has many large farms, but few boast a barn as dramatic as this one. The main farmhouse on the property was built in the 1930s by Louis Kaplan, a local architect who designed three houses in the immediate neighborhood. It stands in four hundred acres of rich farmland, which was home to a herd of cattle. The current owners still have the original breeding record book, with photographs of the animals and their poetic names: "Caumsett Defender," "Cottage Prince Valor," and "Highlander Soldier."

Today, although cows are no longer bred on the farm, the owners have produced their own offspring, who live in the main house, which is situated at the end of a long driveway overlooking the fields and valleys that make up this expansive property. The parents, wishing to retire from the hurly-burly of young family life, decided to convert one of the cow barns up the hill from the main house into living quarters for themselves. Their choice of architect was Michael Graves.

Michael Graves is often mentioned in the same breath as Frank Gehry, Robert Venturi, and Robert A. M. Stern. His controversial architecture, particularly for Disney, has made him excellent copy for newspapers and magazines. More recently, his plunge into home design has given him, as well as the department stores that sell his wares, visibility among many of the homemakers of this country. Yet these ventures have also made him suspect. Is he serious? Is he a dilettante? What is his philosophy?

FACING *The west-facing façade of the barn has twin silos (both original) with pediments and small dormers created by architect Michael Graves. The entrance has a transom and, above it, a balustrade joining the two additions on the upper floors.*

29

The roof of one of the silo wings offers a fine view of the cutting gardens, surrounded by white wooden fences.

Michael Graves was born in Indianapolis in 1934 and drew all the time as a child. "I always wanted to be an artist of some sort," he said. His mother, fearing her son might become the proverbial penniless painter, steered him to a career that would use his talents but also provide him a living—either engineering or architecture. After she explained what an engineer did, he opted for architecture.

He studied at the University of Cincinnati and at Harvard. Here the gods of architecture were Mies van der Rohe and Le Corbusier. "You couldn't look back, you couldn't look forward, you looked at Corbu," he said later. In 1960 he became a fellow of the American Academy in Rome for two years. This period was critical in his architectural life, for here he was first exposed to the great classical and Baroque buildings of that great city. Regardless of the constraints of Corbu, they made a big impression on him.

He came back to assume a position at Princeton University in 1962, where he remained

as a professor of architecture until he retired in 2001. During this time his public career began to blossom. After designing a few residential buildings, he was given his first important
commission—the Portland Building, in Portland, Oregon. This was followed by the Hu-
mana Building in Louisville, Kentucky, the San Juan Capistrano Library, in California, and
the Engineering Research Center at the University of Cincinnati (ironically celebrating the
discipline he had rejected).

By this time Graves's work had taken on its mature form. Its relationship to the early
Modernists was dubious at best. He gave away his bias in remarks he made about the
Denver Public Library, another significant commission. "When we interview for a job like
Denver," he says, "we contrast the traditional libraries from the Baroque to the Rococo with
modern libraries, so many of which seem very icy. Who would want to read a book there?
Don't forsake functionality, but give feelings to it. The use of wood and balconies gives the

*The patio of the original
house is dominated by a
brugmansia, along with
container plants that
change with the seasons.*

The new bedroom wing of the barn has French doors opening onto a patio. It terminates in an octagon whose shape reflects the silos that peek over the roofline.

great Bavarian and Austrian libraries warmth and intimacy. I spent a lot of time in the enormous library in the American Academy in Rome designed by McKim, Mead & White. It never felt enormous because it has shelves perpendicular to the walls, with reading spaces between them, in the style of earlier centuries."

These are not the words of a typical Modernist architect, most of whom would faint rather than mention Baroque or Rococo, or even McKim, Mead & White, in the same context as that of their own work. But Michael Graves has come to be called Postmodern, in that he is happy to "look back." He almost always uses powerful references to classical architecture in his buildings—pediments, columns, arches, and balustrades. His color palette is also historically influenced—terra-cottas, ochres, and pastel blues. He was delighted by architect and writer Colin Rowe, who reinterpreted Le Corbusier by linking him to Palladio. "You think, my goodness, is this possible?" Michael Graves asked rhetorically. "Is the language continuous?"

But then he turned to another direction entirely, one that caused many of his admirers to think twice. He took on the commission of designing two hotels for the Walt Disney World Resort in Florida, and for them he reached into what has often been called "whimsy." The

TOP LEFT *The living room stands on the same footprint as the ground floor of the old barn, only raised to a new height. The beams are original.*
TOP RIGHT *Part of Michael Graves's addition to the barn includes a gallery for the owners' collection of folk and modern art.*
BOTTOM LEFT *The country kitchen is furnished with simple country furniture. The stone mantel was once part of the wall of the tack room of the original barn.* **BOTTOM RIGHT** *A painting by Julie Hefferman dominates the dining room. Doors at each side of it open into the kitchen.*

Hollyhocks bask in the sun in the floriferous cutting garden.

Dolphin Hotel is a turquoise and coral pyramid, with a sixty-three-foot dolphin on top of it and water flowing down the sides. The Swan Hotel is even more startling, its roofline decorated with seven-foot-high swans lined up in a row. Amusing, yes, but the hotel was very alarming to many members of the architectural community who took themselves very seriously and saw this as a travesty of their art.

The owners of this New Jersey barn interviewed several local architects and picked Michael Graves because he had the solution to the problem of keeping the barn intact and making it livable. He listened to their ideas and was immediately sympathetic to their needs. He understood their wish to respect the original nature of the barn, while adapting it so as to be both practical and habitable. The owners have an eclectic art collection, which also had to be accommodated.

As a first principle, the architect used original materials wherever possible. The beams in the living room come mostly from the old barn and other farm buildings, and the stone mantel in the kitchen was once part of the tack room wall. He also appropriated two silos from the farm and incorporated them into his design. The silos now stand at each side of the entrance, like two towers, each topped by a pediment with a small window. The left-hand silo contains a powder room and bathroom above it. The right-hand silo has an elegant spiral staircase that winds upstairs to a guest room. The stairs go up to the roof, where there is a landing and a widow's walk offering a spectacular view over the property.

Michael Graves kept the barn's footprint but changed the height of the structure on that footprint to create new living and art gallery space, creating a wing with French windows that open onto the back courtyard. At the end of the new bedroom wing is an octagon with floor-to-ceiling windows and a conical roof, its curves reflecting the shape of the silos on the front façade. His work here is consistent with his belief that "the language is continuous." The barn is still a barn, but it is also a very elegant piece of contemporary architecture.

The interior of the barn was placed in the hands of Mario Buatta, a distinguished New York decorator who has made a name for himself as a designer of warm, hospitable, often English-influenced rooms. (He is sometimes called "the Prince of Chintz.") For the barn, he eschewed chintz for more rustic materials—linens, wools, oak, pine. He selected muted colors—beiges and grays—that harmonized well with the architecture and the rural context. Above all, the living spaces are comfortable, as the owners had hoped.

During the 1980s, as well as making buildings, Michael Graves also took on the design world, signing an agreement in 1985 with the Italian firm Alessi to produce household objects, such as a teakettle with a bird-whistle spout, and, more recently, chinaware and silverware. Over the years since then he has contracted with other manufacturers to make household items. Today, Graves's designs for alarm clocks, cookie jars, crock pots, Mickey Mouse clocks, and (the latest) digital answering machines sell for a brisk price on eBay. In fact, many Americans think of him as a designer rather than as an architect.

Michael Graves does not see the two as mutually exclusive. He believes that both exterior and interior space should present both the highest standards of design and the greatest livability. "I love the domestic life of buildings, a room, making it human," he declares. With his transformation of this New Jersey barn, he has achieved his goal. While on the one hand he can install seven-foot swans on the roof of a hotel or design a kettle with a bird-whistle, he can also take an old building and, without offending its original function, make it human. "It couldn't be better," say the happy owners, so pleased that they have asked him to design a completely new house for them on adjacent land.

Seibert House

SHORT HILLS, ESSEX COUNTY

The Arts and Crafts movement, originating in late-nineteenth-century England, was a re-action against the effects of the Industrial Revolution, which, in the opinion of many con-temporary artists and designers, had diminished the power of creative individuality in favor of mass-produced products that were often badly made, poorly designed, and—the worst sin of all—a betrayal of the country's native tradition of craftsmanship.

The leaders of the movement, who included the social critic John Ruskin and the designer William Morris, promoted a return to handmade manufacturing and the production of fur-niture, textiles, rugs, and other decorative arts according to traditional methods. They con-veyed the message that everyday objects had an intrinsic natural beauty and simplicity that should not only be encouraged, but also made accessible to all people, rich or poor.

The idea that individual craftsmanship could offer enlightenment through personal ex-pression soon spread to the United States, where one man almost single-handedly assumed the mantle of William Morris and his followers. His name was Gustav Stickley. Originally an architect, Stickley eagerly espoused the principles of the Arts and Crafts movement and in the early 1900s was building simple bungalows and cottages in shingle and cobblestone, in a deliberate return to the plain style of the early settlers. In 1908 he bought 650 acres of wilderness in Parsippany, New Jersey, to be the future home of a community of artisans and craftsmen who would revolutionize the production of furniture and decorative arts in this

FACING *The interior of the house follows the design style of the exterior. The sunroom has both Gothic and semi-Gothic windows, with surrounds made of distressed "natural" wood.*

country. He called his dream "Craftsman Farms," and for ten years his followers made chairs, settees, lamps, ironware, rugs, and fabrics that reflected the simple, democratic principles of their passionate leader.

Sadly, Gustav Stickley was not a good businessman (perhaps by definition no Arts and Crafts proponent should be an efficient money-manager), and gradually the rise of the Modern movement, plus increasingly sophisticated technology in the field of decorative arts, supplanted the demand for individual, handmade, primitive-style objects. When Stickley died in 1942, his work was almost forgotten. Now, however, Craftsman Farms is a National Historic Landmark, and visitors can walk through Stickley's simple cabin home, still furnished with splendid examples of his work.

During the first two decades of the twentieth century, the Arts and Crafts credo that Stickley proselytized so enthusiastically spread like wildfire through the world of art and architecture, and this house in Short Hills, belonging to Mara Seibert, serves as a fascinating architectural example of that period. It was built in 1907 by the New York–based architectural firm of Albro & Lindeberg. Lewis Colt Albro was born in France in 1876 and entered McKim, Mead & White as a student draftsman. Rapidly moving up in the firm, he worked on several important commissions, such as the Columbia University Library and the Man-

hattan home of illustrator Charles Dana Gibson. In 1906 he entered into a partnership with Harrie T. Lindeberg, also a former McKim, Mead & White apprentice, and they soon gained a reputation for their distinguished residential work, establishing their credentials in the field of English vernacular–inspired architecture. After the two split up in 1914, Lindeberg went on to a very successful solo career, his inventiveness and originality compared at the time to giants such as Charles McKim, Stanford White, and John Russell Pope.

For this Short Hills commission, Albro and Lindeberg embraced the principles of the Arts and Crafts movement with characteristic American enthusiasm. The house is constructed of locally quarried stone. Although compact in appearance, it is seven thousand feet square, with a steeply pitched terra-cotta roof, dormers, shutters, a mixture of Palladian and rectangular windows, and a porch entrance. One of the most distinctive features is the exterior woodwork (made of chestnut), which reveals both Gothic and Tudor influences—styles much promoted by the Arts and Crafts designers in England as being authentically English.

The interior of the house is simple, and the space flows freely from one room to the other, with low ceilings and windows opening on all sides to the garden. The sunroom in particular reflects the Arts and Crafts mood of the time, with windows surrounded by distressed "natural" wood carved in the shape of Gothic-style arches.

The rear of the house is in the eclectic Arts and Crafts manner, with dormers, shutters, a patio with Gothic columns, and half-timbering similar to English Tudor houses. The façade is made with locally quarried stone, and the exterior woodwork is chestnut.

The owner has taken great care to respect the architecture and has furnished the interior with fine pieces of the period—Stickley settle and tables, painting by Oscar Bluemner, and lamp by Dirk van Erp.

*A pair of unusual wooden chairs, decoratively carved with balls and
turned legs, invites the visitor to a shady corner of the woodland garden.*

Mara Seibert is well aware of the historic value of her house, and she has furnished it with
pieces that harmonize with the architecture. She has several fine pieces of Stickley furniture, including a settle, two tables, a bookcase, and a server. She also collects Arts and Crafts
pottery, such as Grueby, Newcomb, George Ohr, and Rookwood, as well as early American
Modernist paintings. "I love the house for its Arts and Crafts feel," Mara Seibert says. "And
I love the decorative arts that come with the period. They all work perfectly together."

She appreciates the underlying desire of the Arts and Crafts reformers to retain a connection with simplicity in an increasingly mechanized and impersonal world. Her own work
reflects this: her firm, Seibert & Rice, imports handmade terra-cotta from Italy—individual, beautifully crafted pieces that are as honest as her own private collections. As Gustav
Stickley once said, "The things with which we surround ourselves [should be] truthful, real,
and frank. We are influenced by our surroundings more than we imagine."

Wister Garden

OLDWICK, HUNTERDON COUNTY

This garden is one of the most celebrated in New Jersey. In a space of seventy-five by seventy-five feet, it contains almost every gardener's fantasies, from French *potager* to country orchard, from English cottage garden to majestic herbaceous border, from simple herb plantings to rare horticultural specimens. Surrounded by a white picket fence, the natural extension of a house that dates from the mid-eighteenth century, this little garden is the ultimate expression of the landscape designer's art.

The house belongs to Hannah Wister, who, with her late husband William, spotted it in Finderne, Somerset County, fifty years ago, fell in love with it, and transported it to a rural corner of Oldwick, Hunterdon County, where they had lived for several years. It is a simple clapboard structure, with patios on the east and north sides, shaded by fine stands of trees. The Wisters immediately started planning the garden, which is sited on the south side and enjoys the greatest amount of sun. Divided into eight rectangles, the garden is also divided in the middle by a fence of espaliered apples (mostly Winesap). The classic colonial picket fence that encloses the garden has elegant finials copied from the cornice of the house. The sundial came from Mrs. Wister's grandmother. On the other side of the fence, an orchard marks the perimeter of the landscape stretching away into the still-unspoiled New Jersey countryside.

FACING *The simple mid-eighteenth-century house acts as background to the floral fireworks of 'Red Blaze' roses along the colonial picket fence. The imposing finials were copied from the cornice of the house.*

The garden is divided, like a classic French potager, *into eight rectangles, planted with rows of seasonal vegetables, onions, lettuces, spinach, beets, parsley, thyme, and, later, with tomatoes, broccoli, and peppers. Borders of lavender and beds of roses surrounded by boxwood, with a central sundial, add to the structural elegance of the layout.*

The garden room is really an extension of the garden outside, with standard
geraniums and heliotrope, and wicker furniture upholstered in floral chintz.
Wooden troughs filled with geraniums attract attention beneath the huge windows.

The main architect of the garden is Teo Gonzales, who over the years has choreographed the planting of this small space into two "command performances"—spring and fall. Mrs. Wister spends her summers in Maine, so the garden looks glorious in the spring when she is home, then takes a rest in July and August, ready to explode into bloom again when she returns. In the spring, the vegetables line up in neat rows of lettuce, peas, spinach, onions, and beets. In the fall, the look changes completely with a show of beans, carrots, turnips and parsnips, peppers, broccoli, and tomatoes. Herbs include dill, cilantro, thyme, and parsley.

Gonzales has selected his flowering performers in such a way that there is always something in bloom for her—from rocket, columbine, lupines, poppies, and irises to roses, astilbe, delphiniums, teucrium, lavender, salvia, dahlias, and Shasta daisies. (Some of the English

*Teo Gonzales tends his young seedlings in a small greenhouse,
where he also practices his talent for creating standards.*

and Irish roses have particular sentimental value—they belonged to a neighbor and were lovingly passed on to Mrs. Wister thirty years ago.) Fruiting bushes, such as raspberry and currant, are also ripe for plucking in season. The flower beds are six feet long and four to five feet deep, very large in comparison to most garden borders. The size is why the effect is so spectacular, for he then completely packs them with plants. "I like to see flowers touching each other," he says, pointing to the vivid combinations he has concocted. "And every year it is different."

Although Gonzales has triumphantly organized his plants to time their appearance at the right moment, he has other horticultural passions. One is to create standards—that is, to prune up plants that normally grow as shrubs into miniature trees. He has trained hibiscus, gooseberry, Chinese lilac, geranium, and even heliotrope into standards that decorate the garden with their surprising elegance. "I love making standards," he confesses, eyeing other prospective candidates with enthusiasm. He also admits to a fondness for training unlikely plants along walls in an espaliered form. He maintains a tiny greenhouse where he tends his seedlings, timing their growth so that they can be planted in the garden when they are ready

Another view of the grid-like layout of this tiny garden, surrounded on all sides by the picket fence, with dashes of bright color from annuals and perennials.

to bloom. He spends a lot of time simply pruning—taking out brown foliage, dead-heading, clipping edges, removing tired plants, and replacing them with fresh ones.

This gardener seems to grow with the garden, experimenting, mixing colors and shapes, always aware that he must put on two shows a year. When pressed, he will admit he loves the flower border best. "We propagate everything ourselves," he explains, "so really they are like my children. I watch them grow, urging them to be bigger and better." They eagerly respond, basking in the praise from all those people lucky enough to have visited and admired this astonishing little garden.

The Barn

PRINCETON, MERCER COUNTY

Apart from the famous Delaware River crossing of George Washington with his seriously depleted troops on December 25, 1776, the Princeton Battlefield may be New Jersey's best-known site of the Revolutionary War. Today's Battlefield Park is adjacent to what was known at that time as the town of Stonybrook. The area (1.5 miles from Princeton University) was mostly open farmland, two hundred acres of it owned since 1770 by a Quaker, Thomas Clarke. In 1772 he built a small wood-frame farmhouse on the land, which became, during the fiercely fought Battle of Princeton on January 3, 1777, a retreat for the wounded soldiers. The house still welcomes visitors today in its role as a museum.

The significance of the battle was that, like the Battle of Trenton fought against the Hessians, it proved George Washington's ability to surprise and then defeat British regular soldiers in the field. Washington's leading general, Hugh Mercer, fell during the battle—one of the most devastating so far in terms of casualties—and heroically refused to leave the field until he was sure of victory. He was laid under an oak tree—which until recently stood alone, like a monument, in the field—and then brought to the Clarke House, where he died of his wounds on January 12, 1777. Mercer County was later named in his honor.

In 1835 Charles Smith Olden built a grand Greek Revival mansion, Drumthwacket, a little to the north of the Princeton Battlefield. Fifty-eight years later, in 1893, thanks to a fortune inherited from his father, Moses Taylor Pyne bought the house, extended it with two

FACING *Raleigh Gildersleeve, the architect of Moses Taylor Pyne's picturesque Barn, chose a classical style in brick, with two half-timbered towers (one visible here), tall chimneys, and steeply pitched slate roofs.*

49

wings, and increased the estate's size to 138 acres, including today's Princeton Battlefield Park. Pyne was swept up in the current fad for model farming, an early form of the natural, or organic, agriculture movement, the most inspiring example being Shelburne Farms in Vermont, created in 1886 by the Webb family. Pyne envisioned on his newly acquired land a picturesque landscape in the tradition of Capability Brown and Humphrey Repton in England and Frederick Law Olmsted in the United States, consisting of specially designed out-

buildings, including a Farmer's House, a Dairy, and a Barn, to accommodate his beautifully conceived herds of cattle and sheep. To achieve the utopian cause he espoused, he hired architect Raleigh Gildersleeve to remodel Drumthwacket, as well as to design the new farm buildings. (Moses Pyne was a good patron for Gildersleeve, also commissioning him to build the Pyne dormitories [1896] and McCosh Hall [1906] on the campus of Princeton University.)

Gildersleeve's style is interestingly idiosyncratic. After enjoying a classical Southern upbringing in Charlottesville, Virginia, and Baltimore, Maryland, he trained as an architect in Berlin. There he was exposed to the work of English and German architects, who favored the rustic look of the Arts and Crafts movement. This style seemed suitable in many ways for his client's wishes back in New Jersey. The Barn in particular reflects the various influences of the European-educated architect on his return home. It was sited on the highest point overlooking the Princeton Battlefield, which Pyne had appropriated as pasture for his animals. (Later, white pines were

The courtyard, repaved in red gravel, fronts the north entrance of the Barn, with a six-columned pergola, decorated with wisteria, both added by the present owners. The concrete fountain at the center is original to the building.

planted around the Barn, stretching to the pasture.) The U-shaped layout of the Barn, which would house Pyne's livestock, was classical, with a central courtyard symmetrically framed on each side by stable wings. The architect chose a brick exterior with a timber frame, a slate roof, and two five-story towers of brick, timber, and stucco, half-timbered in the German vernacular mode. The Dairy and Farmer's House were attached to the Barn, which was built in the same style, creating a complex of three functional and interconnected buildings.

The Barn, completed in around 1902, burned down in 1911. According to the local newspaper, all the livestock were saved, but the building was gutted, leaving only the brick walls. Pyne immediately rebuilt it, restoring it, with modifications, to its original state. He died in 1921, having deeded the Barn to his wife, and, at her death in 1939, the estate was inherited by their granddaughter Agnes Pyne. She immediately subdivided the property into parcels and sold the Barn, along with the Dairy and Farmer's House, to Charles Weigel, who turned the complex into a working dairy called the Rockwood Dairy. The dairy ceased operating in the late 1940s, and the Barn remained empty. Meanwhile, Pyne's large pasture,

The interior of the Barn, gutted by Lerner and Fischetti, now boasts a long, open-space living and dining area.
The original beams were restored and the walls repainted. The floor, raised five inches from its original height, is maple.

the Princeton Battlefield, was acquired by the state and turned into a park. In 1960 the Weigels, probably giving in to pressures from developers, sold the property around the Farmer's House for building lots. To accommodate the new housing, a road, Parkside Drive, was constructed alongside the Princeton Battlefield State Park, further separating the Barn from its feudal origins.

During this reconfiguration of the property, the Barn, now down to 1.2 acres of land, was sold in 1960 to Patrick Kelleher, director of the Princeton University Art Museum. The Weigels continued to live in the Farmer's House until 1983, during which time the Barn was required by township law to be separated from the other buildings, causing some of the original structures to be demolished. In June 1995, Ralph Lerner, former dean of the Princeton University School of Architecture, and his wife, architect Lisa Fischetti, bought the Barn from Kelleher's surviving daughter.

As Lerner and Fischetti put it:

> [Our] design intention was to restore the site plan of the Barn back to something that was closer to its original intent. The courtyard has been reopened, and a drive was brought around from the street to the court in alignment with the original estate drive. The front door is now back at the center of the north barn and is directly accessible from the courtyard.... The courtyard has been repaved with red gravel surrounded by a border of pink granite cobblestones and now has the quality of an exterior room, functioning as a point of arrival and gathering.

Originally there were eight sycamore trees and two mature dogwoods in the courtyard, but they were seriously overgrown, so Lerner and Fischetti removed all except six of the sycamores, which have now recovered their health. The circular concrete fountain in front of the Barn is original.

The new owners also transformed the north entrance of the Barn by constructing a six-columned pergola, made of brick to match the Barn walls, over which wisteria trails. They recessed the entry-way to create a double-height porch (plus an exterior window into the kitchen) and put in a door on each side of the porch, one on the left for guests, opening into the living room, and one on the right for family, leading into the kitchen and dining areas.

The interior was radically remodeled. The whole ground floor is open-plan, with the kitchen as the central focus. The floor had to be completely remade and is now five inches higher than the original, covered mostly in maple. The handsome beams were cleaned and restored, and the original brick walls were left as they had been since the Barn was part of the farm. The kitchen was turned around and now faces into the gallery instead of the courtyard, and it is accessible on all sides.

The mezzanine, or gallery, which was once a bridge connecting the two towers of the Barn, has been transformed into a long, narrow library, from which one can look down into the living space below. It is accessed on one side by means of an acid-treated steel spiral staircase, designed by Lerner and Fischetti, and on the other by a wooden staircase original to the Barn. The third floor has family and guest bedrooms and a sitting area leading to a small roof garden at the end of what was once a ramp into the hayloft. The furniture and furnishings reflect the owners' belief that good modern design is perfectly appropriate for a one-hundred-year-old building.

The history of the Barn, and the contemporary use to which it has been put by two talented architects, make for a fascinating spatial and visual exercise. There is no question that this massive brick structure is still a barn, even though it is a fanciful one with its half-timbered towers and elegant wings. By paying faithful attention to its structural lineage, the owners have returned the exterior to its origins as a work of architecture, while converting the interior into a streamlined living space that Moses Pyne (if not his cows) would surely have appreciated.

TOP *In the courtyard, a white horse copied from the Parthenon frieze in the British Museum surveys the scene.* **MIDDLE** *This composition of white-on-white conveys the owners' devotion to architecture.* **BOTTOM** *The Barn has come a long way from the days when Moses Taylor Pyne's cows grazed in this courtyard.*

Castle Howard

The exact date of the house is not known, but on March 3, 1763, Captain William Howard responded to a real estate advertisement in the *Pennsylvania Gazette* for a "new stone house" that refers to this property, which he immediately purchased. The full description of the newspaper story gives a good picture of the property at that time: "There is on said Plantation, lying on the Post Road, between Kingston and Princetown, containing 119 acres, a commodious new stone house, well finished, with a good Stone Kitchen, and a Piazza, a good Draw-well, Barn Stable and Chaise House . . . the whole in good Fence."

Captain Howard named the house Castle Howard, which presumes that he had some connection to the Howards of Yorkshire, whose famous stately home of the same name had been built during the first half of the eighteenth century to the designs of Sir John Vanbrugh on a considerably grander scale than its colonial namesake. (Vanbrugh's Castle Howard had a dome, two huge wings, and a chapel, and it was called a "sublime palace" by Horace Walpole.) There is, however, no evidence of this family connection. Perhaps he had heard of the house's splendid reputation and decided to appropriate it for his own.

Captain Howard bought the house as a bachelor, but in 1769 he married, rather late in life, Sarah Hazard of New York City, and for the years the Howards lived together in the house, it prospered. William Howard seems to have been well off financially; he added approximately twenty acres to the property in 1767, and the place became well known for entertain-

FACING *An elegantly constructed wooden gate invites the visitor to follow the flagstone path into the overgrown garden of the estate.*

ments and parties. During this period, the house was enhanced by a library, antique portraits, and an organ. As evidence of its importance, in 1777 a claim of three thousand dollars (not an inconsiderable sum in those days) was recommended as the value of the estate, the contents of the house, and three slaves sold at auction.

Sadly, Captain Howard did not get to enjoy his property long. A member of the Seventeenth Regiment of Foot, he was a diehard Whig. It is said that over the fireplace in the parlor he wrote, "No Tory talk here." He died during the Revolutionary War just after the Battle of Princeton in 1776 (it is not clear if he was involved in the fighting), and his wife, abandoning the house, returned to England, leaving Castle Howard in the care of their friend John Witherspoon, President of the College of New Jersey, Princeton University's original name. Witherspoon rented the house to Philip Stockton, unofficial chaplain of the Revolution, whose brother Richard, signer of the Declaration of Independence, lived in Morven, another elegant mansion in Princeton. (In recent years Morven and its gardens have been restored and are now open to the public.) Witherspoon later sold Castle Howard to Captain

TOP *The back garden of Castle Howard is a riot of phlox, roses, topiary shrubs, and winding brick paths.*

BOTTOM *The house has been much altered and added on to over the years, but the columns that flank the front entrance and the stucco façade probably date back two hundred years.*

Erkuries Beatty in 1794 (although, thanks to a title dispute, the sale was not completed until 1803).

Beatty was an army officer with an interest in farming. Between the years of 1797 and 1800, he kept a farm diary, consisting of seventy-six pages of daily observations about the workings of Castle Howard Farm. The entries reveal fascinating insights into country customs in the late eighteenth century. ("14 Sept. Rather cloudy day. Isaac ploughed in 3 bushels of rye today . . . Benj. Spreading dung and harrowing down . . . March 17. My brother William went away and in the afternoon I went to Trenton in my Chair . . .")

But Beatty wearied of rural pursuits, and, deciding that country life was too isolating (and perhaps financially unrewarding), he moved into Princeton. After his tenure, Castle Howard changed hands several times. One owner of note was Captain William Lavender, a Quaker sea captain, who acquired it in 1842. Lavender enters the historical legend of the region as a supporter of a Princeton town rally to raise money on behalf of a runaway slave who had been recognized by a Princeton undergraduate as a fugitive from a friend's Maryland plantation. The Fugitive Slave Law of 1850, which required the return of escaped slaves, was in effect, but thanks to successful fund-raising efforts, the local citizens were able to buy the slave's freedom.

In 1866, when the house was once more put up for sale, it was listed as a "farm with 112½ acres on the turnpike between Princeton and Kingston." In 1867 the Reverend H. M. Blodgett bought it. When he died, his will, dated 1875, left the house and land to his executors with income going to his daughter. But the farm at this time was struggling financially, and his executors were forced to try to raise money by renting some of the land as a racing track for trotting horses.

After Blodgett's tenure, the house changed hands again and began to slide into disrepair, a slide that was strikingly well captured in the year 1912 by two photographs in the archives of the Historical Society of Princeton, which record only too well its disastrous state of neglect. If that wasn't evidence enough, in that same year the well-known author and Princeton resident Henry Van Dyke published a ghost story entitled "The Night Call," in which Castle Howard played a major role as a haunted house to which the doctor hero is called on a spectral errand. Called "Castle Gordon" in the story, it is poignantly described as one of the region's "old places," surrounded by "scattered elms and pines and Norway firs that did their best to preserve the memory of a noble plantation. The building was colonial; heavy stone walls covered with yellow stucco; tall white wooden pillars ranged along a narrow portico; style which seemed to assert that a Greek temple was good enough for the residence of an American gentleman." Van Dyke then goes on to describe most vividly its current state of disrepair:

> The clean buff and white of the house had long since faded. The stucco had cracked, and, here and there, had fallen from the stones. The paint on the pillars was dingy, peeling in round

blisters and narrow strips from the grey wood underneath. The trees were ragged and untended, the grass uncut, the driveway overgrown with weeds and gullied by rains—the whole place looked forsaken.

During this unhappy period, Princeton University's rowing crew used the canal at the base of Castle Howard's land for practice, eyeing with longing the property's marshland that they thought might be flooded in order to acquire more water-space. After a failed attempt to dam the Millstone River to form a lake, Andrew Carnegie, famous for his generosity to institutes of higher learning—and for building lochs in Scotland—was appealed to in order to acquire the property. Carnegie agreed to support the plan, but in a typically shrewd Scottish move to keep the price down, the millionaire philanthropist insisted on it being kept a secret. So, in 1903, Howard Russell Butler, a portrait painter and friend of Carnegie's, bought Castle Howard—never intending to live there. "My practiced eye saw this valley and this stream," Carnegie said later in a speech at the formal opening of Carnegie Lake. "And I said, 'O, what a place for a lake—I mean loch,' and Mr. Butler said, 'Yes, for thirty years the students of Princeton have longed for a lake upon which to row and for aquatic sports.' And I said, 'Indeed. . . .' And the spirit moved me and I said, 'Well, Butler, see what you can do, I would like to give Princeton, that Scotch University, a loch.' " (It is said that Woodrow Wilson, then president of Princeton, had asked Carnegie for funds for the university library, to which the great man responded, "Instead of books, I've given you water.")

Castle Howard's modern apotheosis came about through another Princeton University connection. In 1913 A. Thornton Baker and his second wife, Laura, moved to Princeton to be close to his son, Hobart, a Princeton undergraduate, class of 1914, and they bought Castle Howard as a convenient base just outside of town. The Bakers made considerable changes to the house, adding a dining room extension and a large new wing on the north side of the house, which included a studio for Mrs. Baker, an artist, and a small apartment for Hobey (as the student was known). Mrs. Baker is also credited with adding a front garden and formal gardens in the back. In this historic house, Hobey and his friends were frequently entertained by his proud parents.

Hobey Baker (1872–1918) is remembered as Princeton's most famous athlete. His prowess, speed, and grace on the football field and hockey rink made him a local and national hero, taking Princeton into the Ivy League record books. His phenomenal athletic ability, combined with his blond good looks and elusive charm, seemed to epitomize the romantic ideal so vividly portrayed in F. Scott Fitzgerald's novels of the period. (They overlapped at Princeton by one year, Fitzgerald entering as a freshman in 1913.) After college, Baker continued to play hockey, adding to his fame as an athlete. He joined the famous Lafayette Escadrille (the 103rd Aero Squadron) during World War I, and he became as gallant and fearless in the war-torn skies as on the athletic field. But, fated in the classic Greek way, this young god died young.

The smokehouse is built with local stone and sand, dating it to before the construction of the Erie Canal, when cement was first brought to the East.

Just after the Armistice had been signed in 1918, Hobey Baker took up a recently repaired plane for a "last" flight before returning to civilian life. The plane crashed, killing the pilot instantly. While questions remain about the tragedy (some wonder at his seemingly suicidal decision to take off in what was known to be an unproven machine), the legend that almost immediately sprang up of this golden boy, gentleman athlete, and generational role model was so powerful that the *Boston Herald*'s George Frazier wrote in 1962, "He was more miracle than man."

In 1948 Castle Howard was sold to Norton Smith, treasurer of Johnson & Johnson, and, in 1965, his widow sold it to William Augustine, who turned the farm into a development called Castle Howard Court, leaving the original house with two acres. The Pendleton Herrings bought the property that same year, and the family lives there still.

Pendleton Herring, a political scientist and former president of the American Political Science Association, was a member of the Harvard University faculty from 1928 to 1946. For the next twenty years, he was president of the Social Sciences Research Council, and for thirty-five years, president of the Woodrow Wilson Foundation. He also served in the administrations of Roosevelt, Truman, and Eisenhower. "Probably no one in his generation had as great and as varied an impact on social science as Herring," writes Austin Ranney in his entry on Herring in the *International Encyclopedia of the Social Sciences*.

Pen Herring seems to have been the ideal caretaker for Castle Howard and its checkered past. He and his wife, Jill, carefully preserved its character, both inside and out. They filled the rooms with mostly antique English and American furniture that reflects the long history of the house. They worked on the formal gardens, redesigned the pool cabana, and planted two rose gardens, trees, and topiary. "The house has had twenty-two owners and has mostly been sold at auction," Dr. Herring points out. "Its history reflects the issues of the time, particularly the extreme difficulties farmers faced before agricultural subsidies were introduced." Now in the twenty-first century, the farmland has gone, giving the house a new chance to survive.

Today, Castle Howard retains its Greek revival portico and stucco façade. The additions made by the Bakers are still in place, although the house and gardens have been much changed by the next generation of the Herring family. Thus Castle Howard continues to evolve, surviving its long journey from Revolutionary estate to family house, from working farm to literary inspiration, and, like all great houses, still reverberates with the memory of the complex, lively, and tragic figures who have passed through its portals during its two hundred fifty years of existence. 🖋

TOP *The living room has a fine collection of antique furniture passed down through the generations, including the eighteenth-century highboy and gilt mirror over the fireplace.* **BOTTOM** *The hall leading to the plant-filled conservatory is dominated by a Florentine chest inherited by the family.*

Hester Garden

Twenty-five Cleveland Lane was built in 1907 by Charles Peck Warren (1869–1918), assistant professor of architecture at Columbia University. The lane (and at that time it was just a lane) was named after President Grover Cleveland, and it was part of the first subdivision of Princeton town land. Warren chose the Tudor style, with a half-timbered and stucco façade. Tudor Revival was popular with the wealthy middle class at the turn of the century, and other houses built at that time, not only in Princeton, but also in other prosperous communities, have similar architecture. The house was built for landscape artist Parker Mann (1815–1918), who no doubt appreciated the pleasing proportions of the generous entrance porch, steeply pitched gabled roof and dormers, and striking black-and-white exterior created by the architect.

In 1911 Parker Mann sold the house to perhaps its most famous owner, Woodrow Wilson, who had resigned as thirteenth president of Princeton University to become governor of New Jersey (1911–1913). "The little house in Cleveland Lane proved a great success," wrote his daughter Eleanor in a memoir published in 1937. "Though it was furnished, mother added many of our own things—pictures, rugs, and curtains—and filled the house with flowers, so we had a home again and were quite happy."

It was from this house that Wilson left to be inaugurated the twenty-eighth president of the United States. The scene as he was greeted with the news of his triumph was recorded

FACING *From the back of the house, a winding stepping-stone path leads through a woodland garden, planted in a variegated green palette of hosta, ivy, and ferns, to a gazebo.*

At the far end of the garden, Robert Zion's midnight blue circular pool reflects the trees and shrubs in a shimmering double image.

by Maxwell Chaplin, a Princeton undergraduate who went on to be a missionary in China. A parade was formed from Alexander Hall on the university campus, where the election results had been announced, and made its way down to "the little house on Cleveland Lane. The whole college and most of the town turned out. Wilson came out on the little porch and finally got a chance to speak. . . . It seemed so strange that this little group of students and townspeople should be the first to greet the next President at such a simple little house on a side street."

After Wilson left for Washington, the property was bought by Dr. and Mrs. Charles

Williams, who set about turning this "simple little house" into something more substantial. They built a wing that extended the house by a third, making the addition seamless by carefully repeating the architectural format of gables and dormers. They added a glassed-in room at each end of the ground floor of the house and, where bare lawns had been, developed a considerable garden. They put in a rock garden, a rustic arbor, and a rose garden. Dogwoods, Japanese cherries, magnolias, and a border of azaleas added color and shape to the landscape. Dr. Williams was a sometime classics professor at Princeton University, and he and his wife became so well known for their generous hospitality to colleagues and students that the house became known as the "Open Door." (This was also a literal description, thanks to the Williamses' habit of leaving fruit and flowers on the porch ready for visitors.)

The Bright family bought the house from the Williamses in 1964 but were unable to move in for family reasons, and that year Dr. and Mrs. James Hester acquired it from the Brights. At that time Dr. Hester was president of New York University, and, with a family of three small children, they used the house mostly on weekends. From 1975 to 1980, the Hesters moved to Japan at the invitation of the University of Tokyo, returning to the United States when Dr. Hester assumed his new post as president of the New York Botanical Garden, so the Cleveland Lane house did not become their full-time home until almost twenty years after their original purchase.

*Tulips and pansies make a dramatic showing
below the deck at the back of the house.*

The subtle design of Yuji Yoshimura's bonsai and shrubs is set off in the back by a white wall, framed in dark wood. This acts almost like a Japanese screen to separate the property from its neighbor, and it contrasts with the delicately colored pebbles that mark the undulating form of the front perimeter of the garden.

They soon made up for that long absence. Dr. Hester grew up gardening, but he did not find time to practice his interest until he joined the Botanical Garden. "This seemed a wonderful opportunity to live up to my new job," he says. The architecture of the house had been wonderfully preserved during its years of extensions and changes of ownership, a fact that greatly influenced the Hesters' plans for developing the garden.

The house faces directly onto what is now a much-trafficked road rather than a "lane," so the front entrance and porch were not really conducive to horticulture. Whatever gardening was to be done would be at the back of the house. What they inherited there was mostly

The front façade of the half-timbered house on Cleveland Lane shows
the original porch and dormers, with the new extension at the far end.

what the Williamses had contributed—a typical Victorian-style garden, with foundation planting, a red flagstone terrace, a screened porch looking out onto a lawn, a perennial border, a rock garden, and a small brick-paved rose garden to the right of the terrace.

The natural advantages of the garden were obvious—the glorious trees and shrubs that the Williamses had planted, good proportions, and a pleasing slope south and west towards the perimeter. The problems were equally apparent—there was no shape or form to the garden, no vistas to delight the eye, nowhere suitable to entertain outside, and no underlying design to pull the whole space together.

*Dappled light created
by the rhododendrons
and dogwoods falls
on the mysterious
stillness of the pool.*

The Hesters started by making structural changes to the back of the house. They added an upper deck, which gave them a bird's-eye view over the garden. They took away the screened porch and covered up the flagstone terrace with a lower deck that led off the back door into the kitchen, thus solving the problem of outdoor meals.

But the major undertaking was to impose a design that made sense for the whole garden, and for that they turned to the landscape designer Robert L. Zion, designer of many famous gardens, including the Abby Aldrich Rockefeller Sculpture Garden at the Museum of Modern Art. Zion's name will always be remembered fondly by New Yorkers for his trademark invention, the "vest-pocket" garden, his own version being the delightful Paley Park on East Fifty-third Street. (A resident of New Jersey, he lived in a simple eighteenth-century farmhouse in Imlaystown until his death in 2000.)

Like Lawrence Johnston, who created the innovative Hidcote Manor Garden in Gloucestershire, Robert Zion believed that the garden should be a series of "rooms," with the shrubs and flowers as furniture, trees as ceiling, and the lawn as carpet. For the Hesters, he constructed two beds of evergreens, mostly azaleas, laurels, and rhododendrons, lining each side of the sloping lawn to make a narrow "doorway" down to a circular pool at the far end. This created two "rooms," one near the house and the other at a distance. The pool, a Zion mas-

The stone and pebble path that runs parallel to the back deck is alive with color and texture—pieris, azalea, ivy, dogwood, and yucca.

terpiece, is 35 feet in diameter and 5.5 feet at its deepest point, painted black and gleaming at the bottom of the garden like a dark crystal. The Hesters swim in it in the summer, but, unlike most suburban swimming pools, it remains a vital feature of the garden throughout the winter—a shimmering, reflecting lake. The far perimeter of the garden is planted with bamboo, hollies, and rhododendrons, a dense backdrop shutting out views of neighbors and evoking a feeling of privacy.

The excavations produced by digging out the pool were used to build a small hill to the right of the pool, later topped by a gazebo, giving form to the lower part of the garden. The view looking back from the gazebo takes the eye over a lush green carpet of pachysandra and ferns, with shade from European beech trees. (The fern planting was copied from Winterthur, Henry F. du Pont's historic garden outside Wilmington, Delaware.) One of the beeches recently died, and Jim Hester replaced it with two new groups of trees, each consisting of two weeping cherries and a magnolia, "following," as he explains, "Hester's old horticultural adage—always plant in groups of three." In the spring this woodland is alive with Spanish bluebells, another idea from Winterthur.

A stepping-stone path leads one from the gazebo back towards the house. Turning right, one comes upon a secret garden, introduced by a brick path that opens up into a circular

TOP *This stone statue is the focal point of a "secret garden," enclosed in ilex hedges and dominated by an arch smothered in climbing roses and clematis.* **MIDDLE** *The east wall of the front of the house has become a separate "walled" garden, with a central urn on a pedestal, flanked by two lions' heads in octagonal frames, looking out from a green jungle of ferns, azaleas, and evergreen shrubs.* **BOTTOM** *A large bowl on the deck contains a collection of ivy-leaf geraniums.*

In the late spring, the woodland garden is a mass of bluebells,
stretching like a blue carpet towards the horizon.

enclosed space, another "room," lined with evergreens and a neat ilex hedge planted by Robert Zion. In the center of this secret garden is a small statue framed by two English cottage arches decorated with climbing roses and clematis.

But the Hesters had more than one vision in mind. "We had always wanted a Japanese garden," Dr. Hester says. "My good fortune was that the best Japanese gardening talent was right on my doorstep, Yuji Yoshimura, bonsai expert at the New York Botanical Garden."

While Zion was creating his woodland rooms, Yuji Yoshimura came out from New York and made plans for a totally undeveloped part of the garden behind the garage. He established a tea-house/studio in place of the garage, with its own little deck overlooking a tiny rock pool with a bamboo waterspout and floating waterlilies. He built a plain Japanese-style wall along the east side of the property to provide a backdrop for the new garden. In its stark geometry, the black-and-white architecture of the wall harmonized remarkably well with the half-timbering of the house. In front of this wall, Yoshimura worked his magic with local rocks, stones, and plants, and some of his own specially trained bonsai. Without a written plan, he staked out and placed every rock and every shrub in this landscape, siting each element perfectly.

Over the years, the Hesters have continually extended, changed, and improved their garden. "We thought a serious garden should have a good perennial bed," says Dr. Hester. "We had visited gardens in England and felt ours lacked that essential element." So he turned to garden designer Lynden Miller, restorer of the Conservatory Garden and Zoo in Central Park and designer of the perennial garden at the New York Botanical Garden. She and her partner Pepe Maynard borrowed some of the area taken by the Zion shrubbery, while adding more bedding space, to create the deep perennial border that now lines the right side of the vista looking down towards the pool.

For a while, in the front of the house where a new garage had been planned, Dr. Hester created yet another small garden "room" enclosed in trellis, with octagonal windows through which one could see green and white hostas and roses glowing like jewels. That has now gone—for very good reason. In recent years, Jim Hester has taken up an old enthusiasm,

portrait painting. His success has been so great that, in order to fulfill his many commissions, five years ago the Hesters converted the garage into a studio and built a new garage in front of it, again copying the multi-gables, half-timbering, and fenestration in accord with the architecture of the house. Since the new garage took up driveway space used for cars, the little trellis garden had to be sacrificed in order to provide room for parking. However, an echo of its charm is found on the east wall of the front of the house, where, like a large green collage, octagonal frames exhibit lions' heads once used in the film *101 Dalmations*, while a stone pedestal from Little Venice in London holds an urn overflowing with seasonal plants, such as summery verbena and potato vine.

The Hesters continue to make adjustments to the garden as plants grow up and their needs change. "We were lucky to have an old house with some good old-fashioned planting," Dr. Hester says. "But it didn't really belong to us until we started to adapt it. Some gardens don't reveal themselves easily. We can sit on the deck and see the pool, the perennial border, and the Japanese garden all at once." The impact can be quite overwhelming. On one occasion, Arnold Roth, the *New Yorker* cartoonist and onetime Princeton resident, came to a wedding reception the Hesters were hosting for friends. Upon seeing the dazzling displays in the garden, he instantly exclaimed, "Thank God they didn't make him head of the zoo!"

Now, sadly, Robert Zion and Yuji Yoshimura, who played such an important role here, are both dead. "This garden is really a memorial to two great garden designers," Hester says. "Their work here will last as long as we can preserve it."

Scudder Garden

ATLANTIC HIGHLANDS, MONMOUTH COUNTY

It seems strange to many people that New Jersey's official title is the "Garden State." The great highways that slice through the landscape and the vast tracts of manufacturing plants, offices, storage buildings, and housing developments that clutter up the small landmass of this most-populous state give the lie to any credible claim that New Jersey is really a garden.

Yet tucked away in the less built-up parts of the state, protected by unexpected easements and land-use restrictions, gardens of astonishing natural beauty reach back into history and explode on the imagination.

One of these gardens is owned by Richard and Elizabeth Scudder. At the end of a long winding road through woods that spread across the hills north of the Navesink River, it is not far from the eastern tip of the state overlooking Sandy Hook and New York Bay. The site is remarkable—a small valley set down like a jewel at the foot of the Atlantic Highlands. This range of hills is only approximately 200 to 250 feet high, yet it can boast of being the highest point on the coast from Maine to Florida. A huge variety of trees and shrubs rises up here from a natural base of marshes, now transformed into a pond, a stream, and a waterfall.

"When we came here in 1948," explains Dick Scudder, "it was wild woods and swamp. But the potential was evident."

The house, guest house, and garden are approached through dense woods. The buildings are almost entirely concealed by shade trees and large shrubs. The garden opens up behind

FACING *Woodland and swamp in a remote part of Monmouth County have been transformed into an idyllic water and woodland landscape by Richard and Elizabeth Scudder.*

*The pond was made by building a dam around the swamp, where a big flow of spring water
starts one quarter of a mile away. The ducks were rescued from a poultry farm.*

This peaceful corner shows part of the wall with the native stone with which the Scudders started building their house, and Palladian-style windows ingeniously tricked out with panes of mirror instead of glass.

Red and white azaleas show their paces behind the house, along with some of the many shrubs and trees planted by the owners over the years.
A Monet-style bridge traverses a stream that is fed by the pond and winds through the woods to another smaller pond, the entire scene dappled by sunshine.

the main house, consisting of a large, grassy clearing framed on both sides by trees and plants, then sloping down to a large pond that can be glimpsed through narrow pathways and openings in the shrubbery.

Dick Scudder's first love is trees. It was the trees he saw on this untamed land that first captured his heart. In particular he points to a tulip tree on the western side of the garden. It is three hundred years old, and one of the largest and tallest trees in New Jersey. Underneath it he used to find old oyster and clam shells culled from the Navesink River, from the days when Indians sat in its shade and ate their picnics. "We bought the property because of that tree," he says. A partner to this tree grows on the opposite bank, the two standing like guardians of the lawn and plants between them.

A marvelous variety of other trees pay court to this noble couple—sweet gum, dogwood, red maple, hickory, oak, sassafras, Eastern white pine, pitch pine, and black tupelo. One

Proof of the enormous amount of work undertaken each year to create this wonderfully relaxed garden. In one year Dick Scudder planted four hundred rhododendrons.

TOP *A grassy path leads from the lawn behind the house to the pond that stretches out along the bottom of the property.* **ABOVE** *A steep slope rises up in front of the house into a forest filled with important native trees, including hickory, tupelo, oak, and pine.* **RIGHT** *The shed, built like all the outbuildings by the owners, has a pleasing rustic quality that blends in beautifully with the surroundings.*

All gardens should have some surprises. Here a wise man emerges from a tree trunk to watch over his landscape.

species is notably absent—the American chestnut. "This tree was wiped out by blight in 1913," explains Dick Scudder. "It's a magnificent tree, and in the woods above the garden there are hundreds of American chestnut saplings attempting to grow back. But the spore will kill them all."

Walking up the hill behind the house, he points out the native plants that shower the forested landscape with their color and scent, including mountain laurel, azaleas, clethra, and highbush blueberries. In contrast, the garden around the house was almost entirely planted by the owner's own hand. "I planted every evergreen you see," he says, pointing to the massive borders surrounding the clearing that leads down to the pond. "One year I planted four hundred rhododendrons." Sensitive to sun and shade, his plants have responded to the change of climate over the years. "Camellias wouldn't grow here ten to fifteen years ago," he observes. "Now my plants have one thousand blossoms."

As for the pond, Dick Scudder made it himself by building a dam around the swamp, where a big flow of spring water starts a quarter of a mile away. A charming, small, man-made waterfall acts as a focal point to the north end of the garden, the water transforming into a gurgling stream with a Monet-like bridge across it, leading to another smaller pond, mysteriously lit by sun and shadow. The Scudders also built their house, guest house, and pool. "We started with native stone," he says, "but it became too labor-intensive and expensive so we switched to cinderblock."

It is perhaps not surprising that a man who so respects the natural landscape in which he lives should come from a background directly connected to the history of the state. The Scudder family was active in prerevolutionary politics from the beginning of the eighteenth century. Nathaniel Scudder was a signer of the Articles of Confederation, signing New Jersey into the Union in 1777. A colonel in the Revolution, he was the only member of the

Continental Congress killed in action. Richard Scudder, a captain in Queen Anne's War, gave his name to Scudders Falls, land he owned on the border of New Jersey and Pennsylvania. Dick Scudder's great-grandfather was a justice of the Supreme Court of New Jersey from 1869 to 1893.

Dick played his own part in making local and national history. Owner of fifty daily newspapers across the country, he founded the Media News Group in 1983 and was publisher of what was once New Jersey's principal newspaper, the *Newark News*. While producing these publications, he invented the process by which old newspapers are made into newsprint. "I built the first three newsprint recycling mills in the world," he says with justified pride.

That is not the only gesture Dick Scudder has made to environmental protection. He owns sixty undeveloped acres of land on the other side of the road that borders his house and garden. The New Jersey Audubon Society identified seventy-two varieties of birds on this land. Building on the family tradition of public service, Dick has donated the whole property as a conservation easement, which means it can never be developed—a gift to the future of New Jersey that cannot be overestimated.

Meanwhile, he continues to plant, protect, and nurture his wild, colorful, bird-filled, water-loving garden. "The beauty of the place," he says, "is that it's old. It offers the relaxation of a place that has evolved naturally, without being manicured. We just let things grow." He smiles as he admires a huge camellia blossom outside the front door of his house. "The garden offers peace and serenity," he adds. "Something we are all going to be looking for."

FACING *The grassy clearing behind the house is backed by a brilliant display of native plants— dogwood, azalea, and mountain laurel.*

A Private Garden

DEAL, MONMOUTH COUNTY

The history of the New Jersey shore is one of triumph and tragedy, wealth and poverty, fame and insignificance. Like most coastal areas close to big urban centers (in this case, New York and Philadelphia), the New Jersey coast, particularly the northern end, was destined for great things. Long Branch was one of the first and most popular of the towns south of Sandy Hook Bay that was "discovered" by clientele from the big cities to its north and south. As early as 1861 it was visited by President Lincoln's wife, but it was President Ulysses Grant who really put the place on the map, spending many summers there from 1869 onwards. A racetrack and casinos were added attractions, enticing many important visitors, including, as well as several other United States presidents, the major New York and Philadelphia families of the Golden Age (Astors, Goulds, Biddles, and Drexels), famous gamblers such as Diamond Jim Brady, theatrical stars such as Edwin Booth and Lillie Langtry, and the painter Winslow Homer (who did many watercolors of the lovely coastal scenery).

South of Long Branch was another resort that thrived at the turn of the century—Asbury Park, a carefully designed town with trees, green space, and pretty churches. During Long Branch's heyday, many summer visitors also came to Asbury Park, attracted by its lakes, parks, and splendid one-mile-long boardwalk. Both these New Jersey shore towns, however, enjoyed only a brief moment in the sun, so to speak. By the end of World War I and into the Depression, people stopped coming. Damaging storms, organized crime, the

FACING *From the patio at the north side of the house stretches a 190-foot-by-20-foot* allée *of grass, lined with high hedges of arborvitae. A dramatic fountain at the far end closes the vista.*

On the west side of the house, a formal parterre garden displaying beds in geometric shapes,
planted with begonias and defined by clipped boxwood, surrounds a pool with a tulip-shaped fountain
at its center. At the western end, roses tumble over a white trellis with a faux-perspective arch.

abolition of gambling, and the development of other resorts led to economic ruin for these towns, and both of them today are struggling to recover their former glory.

Deal is a small beach community situated between Long Branch and Asbury Park. Named after a town in England, it had originally a population of just over one thousand. It was a simple farming and fishing village until the late nineteenth century, when its neighbors to the north and south began their explosive growth. Their rapid development necessitated that the area be divided into townships (Ocean County, originally part of Monmouth County, was founded in 1849), and the resort towns formed local governments—Asbury Park in 1871, and Deal in 1898.

Deal never assumed the popularity of its more famous neighbors, and perhaps this fact saved it from sharing their catastrophic decline. Early visitors were quick to recognize its modest charms, including Deal Lake, which drew amateur fishermen and summer bathers to its banks. During the boom years of Ocean and Monmouth Counties in the late nineteenth century, many large summer homes were built in Deal, some of them designed by major New York and Philadelphia architects, and thanks to the loyalty of the old guard, and also to newer

families who in later years found the architecture and unspoiled atmosphere appealing, the town is now recognized as one of the richest communities in the state. Privacy is at a premium here, and there are few restaurants or fast-food places to attract the casual tourist. It is a place where the great old mansions still dominate the peaceful, tree-lined streets, many of them carefully restored to their original magnificence. One of these nineteenth-century masterpieces belongs today to a family that has created an ideal garden to go with it.

Their house dates from 1894 and, although not proven, is said to have been designed by Stanford White. It is a classic Victorian gem on an avenue leading off from the ocean. Facing south, defined by a row of fine old trees, it boasts a huge multi-columned porch and elliptical portico, first- and second-floor balustrades and columns, dormers, uneven pedimented rooflines, and highly elaborate carved wood detailing. The owners bought the house seventeen years ago and immediately set about restoring it. The garden had to wait another nine years, but it was worth the wait.

ABOVE *Water spouts from shells that surround the stone fountain at the end of the* allée. *Geraniums add color, and a huge urn at the center gives height to this important focal point.*
FACING *The garden to the east has an English theme: Boxwood hedges enclose flowers typical of an English herbaceous border—roses, lavender, campanula, and salvia.*

At the back of the house were two small cottages, which the owners tore down. They then turned to landscape architect Hermann Schulz to transform the shapeless two-acre plot that remained into a garden worthy of the house it represented. The predictable issue of the garden's location so close to the ocean was the first challenge. Fortunately, although not far from the beach, it is protected from the salty breezes that can be so damaging to plant life. Mr. Schulz also points out that the New Jersey climate has been changing over the years, as it has in so many other parts of the country. Now, he says, one can grow crepe myrtles, camellias, and even Southern magnolias in this part of New Jersey. Thus, a garden in Deal may benefit in the future from global warming as much as others in the region.

Another view of the parterre garden shows the carefully laid-out brick paths,
leading the eye to the far end where a Lutyens bench provides a resting place.

Having established that there would be little problem in persuading plants to grow, Mr.
Schulz made the rest of his design decisions on the strength of the owners' wish to have a
series of garden rooms. First of all, he installed a parterre garden on the west side of the
house. He laid out formally spaced beds in French-style geometric patterns, defined by boxwood and planted with begonias. Brick paths lead the eye to the center of the garden, where
a tulip-shaped fountain plays. On the east side of the house, adjacent to a recent addition,
the English look dominates. (The owners also wanted "something with an English feel.")
Large herbaceous borders planted with roses and other perennials are contained by boxwood hedges, with blue and white as the major color palette.

The most theatrical aspect of the garden, however, is a huge *allée* that stretches out from
the northern patio as far as the eye can see. (The owner's wife had seen in a book an illustra-

tion of an *allée* designed by the great nineteenth- and early-twentieth-century English garden designer, Gertrude Jekyll, and she decided that that was what she wanted.) At the far end, a large stone fountain, decorated with lions and shells spouting water, closes the vista, surrounded by a planting of red geraniums. "I wanted color and movement there," she says.

This striking garden landscape was made possible by the removal of the cottages on the property, and by an elaborate grading job, so that the fountain is now sitting on 10 feet of fill. The *allée* itself consists of a long stretch of grass, 190 feet by 20 feet, lined by two rows of arborvitae, which, as Hermann Schulz points out, are so high that they help emphasize the dramatic perspective. They also play another important role, a role of concealment that could be effective only with hedges this size: behind the western hedge is a basketball court, and behind the eastern hedge a tennis court. (The owners have four sons and a daughter.)

"It is upon the right relation of the garden to the house that its value and the enjoyment that is to be derived from it will largely depend," Gertrude Jekyll wrote in her introduction to *Gardens for Small Country Houses*, first published in England in 1912. One feels that that eminent Victorian would approve of this Deal garden's distinctive design, reflecting so elegantly the architecture of the fine Victorian house to which it belongs. ✿

Parks Garden

MIDDLETOWN, MONMOUTH COUNTY

The Navesink River was originally inhabited by a tribe of the Lenni Lenape Indians. The wide, richly populated river was a breeding ground for oysters, and the Navesink Indians cultivated the shellfish along its banks. The Navesink offered another valuable asset to the early settlers—its shoreline was a pebbly mixture of marl and sand that resisted erosion and provided a good source of fertilizer.

Offering the locals such tangible benefits, the borders of the Navesink remained relatively unchanged through the nineteenth century, except for a certain amount of logging of the woods and continuous farming along the banks. However, the Navesink region, including Middletown and Shrewsbury, gradually became the target of rich New Yorkers seeking country escapes. In 1863 a New York real estate broker called Frederick Guion was the first to put down roots, buying 113 acres near McClees Creek, where he built a fine country house. By the end of the century many others had followed suit, and Monmouth County found itself the center of attraction for wealthy families looking for ocean, river, and farm property to acquire as second homes.

A large package of land along the Navesink was bought between 1906 and 1907 by J. Amory Haskell, an executive in the du Pont Company. His wife was Margaret Riker, as in Riker's Island. (Her mother was a Jackson, as in Jackson Heights—these early families found themselves destined for posterity.) Margaret Haskell's brother was Samuel Riker, Jr., a

FACING *The picture-book setting of this garden is shown here to spectacular effect, with the fountain playing on the pond, delicately swaying grasses in the foreground, and a bank of prolific pink roses underscoring the vista to the Navesink River.*

An antique ram's head from Europe rises up proudly from a shroud of ivy. The carved stone structure works as a fountain, water trickling into the shell beneath the foot of the pedestal.

The rear of the house, facing the river, has large bays ornamented with elegant wrought-iron balustrades and window panels. A large hydrangea bush protects the patio from prying eyes.

lawyer, who also liked the Middletown area, and in 1915 he built Holly House, the house on Navesink River Road that currently belongs to David and Lisa Parks and their family. (Riker, with architect Leon Cubberly, had already built a much larger house, Overlook Farm, that is now the Navesink Country Club.)

Holly House is in the French architectural style, which comes as no surprise when one learns that Samuel Riker was born in Paris in 1868. The house is situated at the end of a long driveway, its south façade facing the river, with a west-facing conservatory. The house is built of brick, with a fine front door, portico, and wrought-iron staircase. Dormers add to the French feeling of the architecture. One of the most appealing and unusual aspects of the exterior is the ornamental wrought-ironwork decorating the west and south sides.

After the departure of the Rikers, perhaps the most famous owners of Holly House were Nicholas G. and Helen Rutgers, scions of the Rutgers family who founded the university in New Brunswick in 1825. (Nicholas Rutgers named the house "Holly House," not only for its trees but also because he called his wife Holly.) Nicholas Rutgers bought the house in 1950 and lived in it in the grand style as befitted his position. Thus the carriage house and garage are situated halfway down the driveway, an acceptable distance for the Rutgers staff

to fulfill their duties, although totally impractical today. (Lisa Parks points with amusement to the mother-of-pearl call buttons, still in place at the foot of the main staircase of the house, to summon the butler.) The Rutgers family were also keen plantsmen, and the house became known for its lush gardens. Sadly, Mr. Rutgers died suddenly a year after purchasing the house, but Mrs. Rutgers remained in the house until her death in 1961.

In line with the other early Middletown mansions built along the Navesink River, the essential architectural and aesthetic element of Holly House is its spectacular site, and the garden takes full advantage of its unique setting. The garden area today expands across just under four acres on all four sides of the house. Although no plans for the original landscaping remain, two large hollies at the house's entrance have established their provenance, thanks to Lisa Parks's own research into the garden's history. One of the men working on the grounds discovered an old sign. It read, "Holly House," confirming the name bestowed upon it by Nicholas Rutgers in honor of his wife and the eponymous hollies in the landscape. Other important trees include a specimen beech tree, three weeping willows overlooking the pond, a bamboo planted by Nicholas Rutgers's son that grew to approximately fifty feet, and the largest deciduous larch tree in New Jersey, checked annually by the state.

David and Lisa Parks embarked on a comprehensive planting program to improve the garden. They planted 160 pink Meidiland rose bushes along each side of the driveway. On the east side of the house, they created a long bed lining the ellipse of the entryway and planted it with a dramatic summer color scheme consisting of bright red cannas and white snapdragons. The pond, which is very old (the stone coping is very fragile and crumbles easily), is fed by underlying natural streams coursing from the neighboring golf course. Standing on its northern edge, one enjoys a stunning view that reaches to the opposite banks of the Navesink River. A subtle planting of grasses on the borders of the pond acts like a feathery scrim through which a fountain plays. A bank of pink roses, rising up from a low stone wall, provides color and shape to the vista and acts as a screen concealing the pool area beyond. On the horizon, the river creates an elegant counterpoint to the rippling water of the pond.

In contrast to this dazzling display of flowers, shrubs, and waterworks, the conservatory side of the house offers a completely different experience. A simple door through the brick wall to the right of the entryway invites the visitor into a peaceful, shady retreat, with a small lawn overlooked by banks of perennials. Rising above a backdrop of ivy, a fountain in the form of an antique ram's head allows water to trickle gently into a stone shell nestling in the greenery below.

The design of the back of the house suggests yet another kind of space. Sited high above the riverbank and exposed to the glorious view below, this area is devoted to entertaining. A bluestone patio, furnished with tables and comfortable outdoor furniture, extends from French doors leading out of the living and dining rooms. (The ground-floor space is designed so that, with the front door open, the river can be seen from both sides of the house.) Large shrubs such as hydrangeas line the edge of the patio, providing a sense of privacy for family and friends. The garden then drops off dramatically in the form of a rocky hillside going down to the river. Meandering stone paths and walls, planted with rock-loving and wind-resistant plants, draw the eye down towards the water, where a long jetty stretches out into the middle of the river for boats and swimmers.

Gardens near water are often designed under the misapprehension that they must compete with the natural advantages of the site. In the Parks garden, the variety of the several spaces surrounding the house and the striking contrasts in color, texture, and structure of the plantings create a brilliant ensemble setting for the river. While, as the poet Robert Bridges observed, "Nature is loth to yield to Art her fair supremacy," in this case the man-made landscape works in perfect harmony with the beauty of its surroundings.

TOP *The house is designed in the manner of a French chateau. Fine trees, including this one, the largest deciduous larch in New Jersey, guard the property between the house and the road.*
BOTTOM *The beautiful and unusual wrought-iron ornamental decoration of the windows and roofline was meticulously restored by the present owners.*

Grotta House

MORRISTOWN, MORRIS COUNTY

The decision to build a house poses huge questions. Where? How big? And most important, what style? For Mr. and Mrs. Louis Grotta, certain conditions were already in place. They had found a lovely seven-acre property on the outskirts of Morristown, in rolling New Jersey countryside. Now that their children were grown, they were leaving behind a traditional family house in Maplewood and looking for a different kind of space for themselves. Moreover, they owned a growing collection of contemporary crafts in ceramic, fiber, and wood, mostly created by American artists, for which they wished to provide an appropriate setting.

The Grottas had known architect Richard Meier since childhood, and one day they asked him whom they should choose to build their house. "He said he'd do it," Sandy Grotta recalls, still a little amazed. So Richard Meier took on the commission and between 1984 and 1989 produced a house that was so beautiful and elegant that it was chosen for the cover photograph of the architect's own book, *Richard Meier Houses*, published in 1996.

By this time, Richard Meier's work had achieved worldwide recognition. His career, unlike that of many architects, was remarkably trouble-free. He had always dreamed of being an architect, and, after a brief stint with Skidmore, Owings & Merrill, he worked for three years under Marcel Breuer, whose commitment to the International Style was greatly to influence the young American. The Smith House on Long Island Sound in Connecticut was the first house Meier designed that indicated the architect was finding his own voice. Built

FACING *The soaring central cylinder of Richard Meier's design is made of glass, set in a gleaming cylinder of white enameled porcelain panels.*

103

in 1967, this "sleek white building" was the first in a line of sleek white buildings, in the words of architecture critic Paul Goldberger, that culminated in the "sleek off-white" Getty Center in Los Angeles, completed in late 1998. By this time, many observers could identify Meier's signature style—apart from the sleek whiteness, there were the Modernist curves and tubular detailing reminiscent of the great Art Deco ships of the 1920s, the extensive use of glass, and the lyrical interplay of surface and space.

Meier admits that Le Corbusier and Frank Lloyd Wright were great influences on his work. "Fallingwater had an electrifying effect on me," he said later, "more than any other building I had seen." Meier's other driving passion is the relationship between the house and its surroundings. "What was important to me . . . having read all Frank Lloyd Wright,

In the sunken living room, the teak card table and coffee table are by Joyce and Edgar Anderson, the walnut chairs are by Hans Wegner, the leather sofas are by Mies van der Rohe, and the ceramic on the coffee table is by Toshiko Takaezu. The basket is by John McQueen.

ABOVE *The west-facing façade of the house shows the seamless line that leads the eye from the house through the archway to the landscape beyond.*
RIGHT *On a shelf in a corridor leading off from the master bedroom is a collection of wooden bowls by Bob Stocksdale.*

*The light, flat planes of the interior layout of the house offer ideal
exhibition space—here a plate and a tall ceramic tree by Toshiko Takaezu.*

as a student, was the extension of interior space into the landscape." All of Meier's work
reflects this abiding interest. Paul Goldberger, describing one of Meier's most recent works,
the United States Courthouse and Federal Building in Central Islip, Long Island, completed
in 2000, finds apt expression for Meier's latest masterpiece: "It is a breathtaking sight, em-
bodying one of modernism's great fantasies, the notion of the building as a pure and perfect
object set, like a piece of sculpture, in nature: the dream of the machine in the garden."

The Grotta House embodies this concept brilliantly. Set in a seven-acre sloping field, the
house is backed to the north and west by a fringe of trees and looks south and east over the
hilly landscape of north-central New Jersey. Approaching it from the road, the visitor is
struck by the pristine cylindrical curves of the front façade, set in a gleaming skeleton of

white enameled porcelain panels, rising from the distant green lawn. The back of the house is made of gray concrete blocks, offering a striking contrast of texture to the smooth, sleek front.

Yet while spectacular in appearance, the house is surprisingly compact in size. Thanks to its sloping site, it is designed on several levels. The height of the building is only twenty-four feet, with a sunken living room, a steeply raked staircase, two bedrooms, and glass windows looking out on all sides. "In fact, the number of rooms is the same as in our house in Maplewood," Sandy Grotta explains. "I didn't want a mega-house." The interior is designed around two central axes radiating out into the garden. One is the entry at the east side of the building that connects the parking area and garage to the house. The other extends from the second floor of the interior out across a bridge, linking it to the gentle hillside to the north. A further extension to the west side of the house consists of a paved path leading to a rectangular archway, freestanding like a piece of abstract sculpture, that frames the landscape beyond. All these architectural devices serve the same purpose, to allow the space to flow seamlessly from the inside out in a continuous relationship—a "machine in the garden."

A corridor leading from the front door opens into the sunken living room, which faces south, with floor-to-ceiling curved windows, white tubular columns, and exterior railings that give one the feeling of being on the prow of an ocean liner. On the west side of the living room, at ground level, are the dining room and kitchen areas, and a bedroom. On the second floor are the master bedroom suite and studies. A rear door facing north opens onto a bridge with white railings—again the nautical imagery is irresistible—like a ship's gangway, connecting the house to the grassy landing and wooded area beyond. A basement houses the Grottas' extensive library and office equipment.

The furniture and furnishings are carefully calibrated to the architecture. Sandy Grotta

is an interior decorator and had special requirements for her rare collections. Thus the house, as well as being a family home, is also, in a sense, an exhibition space, but without the formality that notion implies. "The objective was not to create a museum," explains Lou Grotta. "The only thing on a pedestal in our house is my wife." Natural light from the windows embraces the many ceramic, basket, and wood pieces throughout the house, by such artists as Shiela Hicks, John McQueen, Lenore Tawney, and Peter Voulkoes.

The furniture and fabrics blend impeccably with the subtle lines and colors of these objects. There are several types of furniture: built-ins designed by Richard Meier, freestanding pieces by craft artists such as Sam Maloof and Wendel Castle, and classic Modernist examples by Charles Eames, Mies van der Rohe, and Hans Wegner. The ceramics and woodwork of the Grottas' longtime friends Toshiko Takaezu and Joyce and Edgar Anderson (all New Jersey natives) appear in nearly every room. Each object relates well to the others in these striking surroundings.

"I care very much for all these artists," Sandy Grotta says. "Richard knew what had to be done for them." With a body of major international work under his belt, Richard Meier put into this modest private residence all the skills at his disposal, and the result is a great building on a human scale. "You cannot have form in architecture which is unrelated to human experience," he told an audience at the Royal Institute of British Architects in London in 1988, "and you cannot approach an understanding of experience, in terms of architecture, without a strongly sensuous and tactile attitude toward form and space. The site invites the architect to search out a precise and exquisitely reciprocal relationship between built architecture and the site." Meier said this at the time he was building the Grotta House, and one cannot help but feel he was thinking of this New Jersey gem, which now stands as a shining example of his deepest-felt artistic beliefs.

Ellman House

Long Beach Island is an eighteen-mile-long barrier island four miles off the Ocean County mainland. It is very narrow—approximately one half-mile wide—so that many of the residents of the small towns that dot this strip of land can see both the ocean and the intracoastal waterways out of their bedroom windows. The other unusual feature of Long Beach Island is that it is accessible by only one route—the Manahawkin Bay Bridge. This limited access gives the island its special quality of exclusivity and isolation, which some compare to Cape Cod.

The island was originally discovered by Dutch explorers. In the eighteenth century it became a popular center for New England whalers, thanks to its position near the migratory routes of whales. By the end of the nineteenth century, tourism had replaced whaling, along with the occasional activity of pirates, according to popular legend, who used deceptive lights to waylay ships on their way to and from New York and plunder them. Today few pirates seem to ply their trade, with pleasure boats and swimmers instead populating the beaches in the summertime.

The island's main road, Long Beach Boulevard, connects the small resort towns, which are spaced a few miles from each other. The southernmost town is Holgate, and at the tip of the northern end is Barnegat Light, a famous tourist attraction. The lighthouse, known as "Old Barney," was originally built in 1834 and replaced by the present tower in the years of

FACING *Nobody would mistake this house for a typical New Jersey shore beach cottage. Architect Robert Venturi, who designed it in 1969, made quite sure of that.*

*Venturi's plan called for a small, square box, flat-roofed, with a tower at
one corner and a line of crenellated glass doors and windows facing the ocean.*

One of the extraordinary elements of this house is the huge round window, cut almost in half,
which dominates the western façade and interior staircase from the ground to first-floor levels.

*An unusual zigzag line of windows and French doors defines
the roof exposure, which is also a patio with a view of the ocean.*

1857 and 1858. It is 165 feet tall, standing high above a small state park of just over 31 acres.
Barnegat Light served an invaluable purpose to mariners for over sixty years, sending out
its white warning beam over a radius of thirty miles, until in 1927 a more modern lightship
stationed nearby rendered it obsolete. Today visitors may climb the 217 steps to the top of
the lighthouse and view the gorgeous scenery stretched out below.

Just under 4 miles from Barnegat Light and almost within its shadow is the northernmost
resort town of Long Beach Island, Loveladies. "Loveladies" is by any reckoning a strange
name for a town, but Long Beach Island boasts several others that raise an eyebrow—for instance, Ship Bottom and Harvey Cedars. Legend offers various reasons for these odd names,
the most romantic being the story of the beautiful Spanish woman found inside the hull of

Venturi found the surrounding banal landscape, the "environment of utility poles" as he called it, an essential contributor to the boxy robustness of the beach house.

a boat that was washed up on the shore, bottom up, in the early 1800s, the lone survivor of a wreck off Barnegat Shoals, the spot being thus identified forever after as Ship Bottom. The origin of Loveladies is more prosaic—it is named after one Thomas Lovelady, a hunter who spent a lot of time in the area shooting ducks.

Loveladies offers a more significant claim to fame than this long-forgotten sportsman. In 1962, a huge storm flooded the town and destroyed most of the houses that had been constructed there, leaving a tabula rasa on which future architects might sketch their Modernist dreams. Not surprisingly, therefore, this "virgin" town has attracted many cutting-edge architects, who find the lack of traditional context here both exhilarating and liberating. Architect Michael Ryan, who is currently building several houses in the area, explains that

Loveladies is like a campground, without a history or identity, an extension of the idea that all barrier islands are "placeless places, context-free, neither urban nor suburban."

His words echo the controversial philosophy of Robert Venturi, master of the vernacular, agent provocateur of Postmodernism, and author, with his wife Denise Scott Brown, of the groundbreaking 1972 book, *Learning from Las Vegas.* In this book, architects were urged to break away from historicism and aestheticism and consider commercial and industrial buildings, along with roadside signs and advertisements, as relevant design styles for the contemporary world. "The ordinary and the familiar can become surprising and inspiring," they declared, and, "the only thing worse than vulgar urbanism is tasteful urbanism." Such statements, needless to say, raised hackles both in and out of the profession, and all eyes were on the houses that Venturi and Scott Brown actually built. So when they took on the assignment

ABOVE *The open-plan living space on the first floor is illuminated by a section of the pie-shaped west window.*
RIGHT *The interior of the corner "tower" turns out to be a protective seating area, offering privacy, as well as the ocean view.*

Defiant from any angle, the huge street identification of the house—a five-foot-tall number 9—looms over an equally outsized twenty-four-foot-wide stoop.

to design a small summer house for the Lieb family in Loveladies in 1969, it was no small matter. The place has never been the same since.

The house is within a few hundred yards of the shore, and its rear half is actually located in Loveladies, and its front half in Barnegat Light, so it already has a provocative provenance. It is located on a small street lined with a few shrubs, small lawns, and rows of telephone poles—in other words, in a background of typically unplanned, modest suburban plots backing onto each other and crawling out towards the ultimate destination, the beach. Venturi described his design for the Lieb House as a "shed" (one of his favorite words, the "decorated shed" being one of his descriptions of modern architecture that reflected his belief in visual and symbolic paradoxes). "It's a little house with a big scale," said the architects after its completion, "different from the other houses around it but also like them. It stands up to, rather than ignores, the environment of utility poles."

In appearance it certainly is different from its neighbors—it looks like a small, square box, flat-roofed, flat-sided, with a strangely sliced-up round window inserted in the western façade. The whole structure is wrapped in asbestos shingles with wood grain relief (once the indigenous building material on Long Beach Island, according to the architects), the bottom half gray and the top half painted white.

Of course, the initial impression of a square box is highly deceptive. In an amusing description of the house by Robert Venturi and John Rauch, with Gerod Clark, that appeared in an architectural monograph devoted to the work of Venturi Scott Brown and Associates, they write, "its unconventional elements, when they do occur, are explicitly extraordinary." Indeed they are. The first element that is explicitly extraordinary is the roofline, which, although appearing box-like, is in fact broken up like a giant crenellation on two sides, allowing the roof to become a living space, with views of the ocean. Another unusual element is the huge, round window, cut almost in half, that dominates the west-facing side of the house. A further surprise is provided by the oversized front entrance, with a twenty-four-foot-wide stoop (as wide as the width of the house) spreading out along the street, narrowing to three feet at the front door. And what could be more explicitly extraordinary than the startling five-foot-tall house identifying number, defying all modesty?

The interior of the house has more subtle innovations. Although the building is square, all the rooms are designed with the walls slightly at an angle, avoiding a boxy feel. All four bedrooms are on the ground floor. The washer and dryer, usually off a bedroom upstairs, are installed in the hall, thus freeing space upstairs. The second floor consists of a large, open-plan living space that includes a kitchen, a dining area, and a fireplace. "Stepped" French windows on the east side of the room open onto a deck. There is an entrance at the east side of the house with an outside shower, again a practical design element, so that people coming from the beach may shower off before entering the house. Every angle and corner was meticulously measured for maximum practicality, as well as aesthetic effect. "Good architecture involves fractions of inches as well as ideas," says Robert Venturi.

For the Liebs, who commissioned the house in 1969 at a cost of thirty-one thousand dollars, it was a challenge, to say the least. But although it was unconventional, they quickly pointed out its genuine practicality as a beach house. "It's a real dumb house, just a box, but it's gorgeous," Judy Lieb said. For the neighbors, who watched this strange object going up, it was more than dumb, it was shocking. Most of them understood a summer house to be what they lived in—Cape Cod–style bungalows or wooden beach cottages. Venturi's "shed" was not at all appropriate for the residents of the mild, middle-class streets of Loveladies, however firmly the architect declared it to be "different from the other houses, but like them."

"Good art cannot be universally liked in its time," Venturi asserts. "The issue is, do the right people hate it?" According to Mrs. Lieb, people hated it so much that they stopped talking to her, and at some point, she moved elsewhere. The house, however, remained, a defiant statement of radical architecture, until Leroy and Sheila Ellman, both devotees of modern art and architecture, bought it in 1979 and set to work to restore Venturi's small masterpiece. "Architecture is the most fragile of the arts," Robert Venturi has pointed out, "even more than works on paper, which people know must be treated with special care."

The Ellmans, deeply respectful of this fact, were extremely careful with their restoration work. They consulted sketches of the house and were in correspondence with Venturi himself before making any changes. Windows, a balcony, and rotting cedar siding were replaced, and the new owners removed a gutter and downspout that spoiled the appearance of the exterior of the house. They added windows in the living room over the banquette to bring more light into the space, and they enlarged the oval glass inset in the front door. Otherwise, they are proud to point out that it is almost exactly the house that Robert Venturi built over thirty years ago.

Whenever there is a show of the work of Venturi Scott Brown Associates, Number 9 is part of the exhibition. The owners are delighted to share their pleasure in this remarkable piece of architecture. "It has been called a 'banal box,'" they say. "But for us it is a consummate summer house. Its simplicity makes it so."

Abel and Mary Nicholson House

SALEM, SALEM COUNTY

For an inspired moment in New Jersey's architectural history, builders in southern New Jersey produced a number of houses decorated in patterns of vitrified brick that not only dazzle the eye but also stand as a testament to the talent of the eighteenth-century craftsmen who created this extraordinary work.

Salem County was founded in 1675 and is situated on the southwest corner of the state, boasting a population of less than 65,000—the lowest population and lowest density per mile in New Jersey. How these dazzling patterned-brick houses came to be built here (and in several neighboring counties) is not known, but the style clearly became fashionable in the region in the early eighteenth century and was widely copied by settlers as they moved into the area. These farmers probably employed the same team of bricklayers as they continued to build. Unique in its originality and playfulness, the patterned-brick house became representative of early colonial New Jersey architecture and one of the state's most important legacies.

The dazzling designs were formed by the vitrifying, or burning, of plain red brick so that the color turned from red to a blue or blue-gray. The brick was then inserted into the wall on its end, rather than on its side, thus allowing the designer to create elaborate checkerboard patterns in the regular brickwork, typically on the gabled end, of the building. The technique originated in medieval England and took hold in the early eighteenth century in

FACING *The so-called "diaper" pattern, of repeated and interlocked units of design, is typical of the vitrified brick style. The date of the house, 1722, is proudly displayed beneath the peak of the gable under the roof.*

The dazzling intricacy and subtle colorations exhibited in this example of vitrified brickwork could have been created only by a master mason.

This outstanding example of early eighteenth-century New Jersey architecture stands alone, literally and metaphorically, like a jewel box in the rare isolation of Salem County.

southern New Jersey, where at least one hundred houses at one time displayed this unusual design feature. According to art historian Paul Love, the style was first exhibited in the Joseph Darkin House in Salem County in 1720, and it "became an expected decoration on almost all houses after that date and continued until 1792." (It should be noted that the number of brick houses still standing is thanks to their hardy material; far more houses of the period were built of wood but did not survive.)

The Abel and Mary Nicholson House is dated two years after the Darkin House, both of them originating in the same region of Elsinboro Township, outside Salem. The patterning is inserted into the east gable, where the "diaper," or pattern of repeated and interlinked geometric units of design, is five diamonds wide and seven diamonds long in the widest area of

LEFT *The south side of the house offers a subtly colored palette of grays and reds, with the initials—probably those of the mason—carved into one of the central bricks.* BELOW *The dramatic diaper pattern appears only on the east side of the house. It is five diamonds wide and seven diamonds long in the largest area of the gable.*

As is evident from the change in brickwork, a western wing was added later, in 1859.
The flight of stone steps to the entrance of the older wing is thought to be original.

the gable. The diaper diminishes as the gable narrows towards the roof, culminating in the date of construction, 1722, and above it a "V" shape at the apex of the gable under the eaves.

Unlike some of the other houses of the period, the front and rear façades of the Nicholson House are also decorated with vitrified bricks, in each case creating a geometric checkerboard of light and dark patterns. The skill in creating the perfect geometry on these façades, plus the carefully placed brick quoins at each corner of the house, defies description. The letters carved on a brick on the south side of the house are perhaps the initials of the owners, or more likely those of the mason, a fitting permanent record of one man's brilliant craftsmanship. (Owners' initials were more typically incorporated into the main diaper of the gable and set in big letters, emphasizing their status.) Later houses exhibit more elabo-

*Another view of the south façade of the house shows the
two wings and the dormers, which were also added in 1859.*

rate and intricate patterns, in particular the Dickinson House, near Alloway, also in Salem
County, which is a riot of diamonds, floral patterns, a date that stretches over the widest part
of the gable, and equally large initials (in this case belonging to the owner) towards the eaves.
But the Abel and Mary Nicholson House, which stands alone in a field, isolated, seemingly
untouched by civilization, is ideally suited to the austere perfection of its brickwork.

Thanks to the research of Ronald E. Magill, president of the Salem County Historical
Society and a regional architectural historian, we know that Abel Nicholson was born on
May 2, 1672, and at the age of three he sailed to America with his parents and four siblings.
His father, Samuel, originally of Nottingham, England, had been deeded five hundred acres
in Elsinboro by a friend, John Fenwick, plus a sixteen-acre lot in Salem. (It was customary
to transfer land consisting of both rural acreage and a town lot.) Fenwick's lot is where the
Salem Monthly Meeting of the Society of Friends was founded in 1681 and where the fa-
mous Salem Oak, believed to be over four hundred years old, still stands. It is said that John
Fenwick made a treaty with the Lenni Lenape Indians under this tree in 1675. Abel Nichol-

son married another Quaker, Mary Tyler, in 1693, and they had eight children. In 1722 they built the house that bears their name today.

While additions have been made to the house, most notably a brick wing with pedimented dormers at the western end of the house, built in 1859, the miracle is that both the exterior and the interior of the eastern end have remained untouched. "This half of the dwelling has never seen electricity, central heat, or any amenities of twentieth-century life," says Mr. Magill. He also points out that the house's earliest portion is flanked by two massive chimneys of exceptional design. He adds, "Stone steps—believed to be original—lead to the south entrance."

The wall that divides the two interior rooms in the earliest section is a single beaded board, and most interior hardware, hinges, locks, mantels, and trim are original. There is also an unusual "writing" closet with a built-in writing surface on the ground floor, originally illuminated by a window in the gable, said to be common in seventeenth-century dwellings in England and America, allowing

Both the brickwork and the original chimneys are of exceptional interest. The house was never invaded by electricity or central heating, thus maintaining its pristine authority.

for speculation that literacy was reaching even these modest households by the early 1800s. A small closet on the second floor has a bench, perhaps for reading and working. The nineteenth-century addition has also much of its original detailing, including a fireplace measuring over five feet wide. Ron Magill, declaring that it is one of only twenty-five surviving patterned-brick houses in Salem County, says that of all of them, the Abel and Mary Nicholson House probably contains the most intact, original interiors.

Other architectural experts are equally respectful. "In terms of its extraordinary architectural integrity and its well-documented associations with the earliest Quaker settlements in the region, I see the Abel and Mary Nicholson House on a par with the Fairbanks House in Dedham, Massachusetts, and Bacon's Castle in Surry County, Virginia," writes Bernard L. Herman, professor of art history at the University of Delaware. "[This house is] one of America's best time capsules of eighteenth-century life," agrees Carl R. Lounsbury, architectural historian at the Colonial Williamsburg Foundation.

These comments were part of a body of evidence collected by Ronald Magill in order to nominate the house for landmark status. His efforts were successful, and in 2000 the Abel and Mary Nicholson House was afforded National Historic Landmark status. Coming upon this fascinating house, proudly standing in a secluded Salem field far from the noise and bustle of New Jersey's arterial highways, only recently vacated by its last, longtime owners, the visitor can only marvel at the ingeniousness and aesthetic sense of these early settlers and their talented builders and masons.

Faircourt

BERNARDSVILLE, SOMERSET COUNTY

The discovery of the Somerset Hills, spearheaded by architect George P. Post, who built his house, Claremont, in Bernardsville in 1895, and C. Ledyard Blair, who decided to build his French mansion, Blairsden, in Peapack, even before the railroad reached the area, was quickly and enthusiastically taken up by their New York industrialist colleagues, who, like them, had either earned or inherited fortunes from the explosive growth of the mining, banking, building, and transportation industries that took place at the end of the nineteenth century.

In 1896 Henry R. Kunhardt, a shipping magnate, decided to join what was becoming known as the "Mountain Colony"—after the Bernardsville Mountain on which many of these estates were being built. (It was also, rather appropriately, sometimes called "Bankers Mountain.") Perhaps admiring the example of his neighbor in Peapack, Kunhardt commissioned the same architects, Carrère & Hastings, to design a country retreat for him. If he was expecting the same kind of French extravagance that they had produced for Blair, he was in for a surprise. For this client Carrère & Hastings abandoned their usual French or English repertoire for something more exotic—a 15,000-foot, three-story, Mediterranean mansion, with terra-cotta tile roofs, arches, seven chimneys, and a stucco façade. Two long east-facing loggias extend from the central wing, both of which were originally open. The loggia at the south end of the house has now been enclosed and has the feel of a conservatory. The

FACING *Faircourt was completed by Carrère & Hastings in 1899. The architects chose a Mediterranean style of architecture for their client, with the east-facing stucco façade showing the loggias, Palladian-style windows, and tiled roof typical of the genre.*

Every decorative element of the library/ballroom of Faircourt shows its quality —the herringbone parquet floor, the oak paneling, and the exquisite coffered ceiling picked out in gold. A grand piano and French eighteenth-century gilded commode with claw feet add distinction to this most glamorous of rooms.

overall impression of Faircourt is of a greatly expanded version of the Spanish and Italian villas that had flourished for many preceding centuries all over Europe.

Perhaps the most appealing design feature of the house is its interior courtyard, so familiar in Mediterranean layouts, that boasts a grand front door with ornately carved Corinthian columns and a pediment topped by a balustrade, irregular-sized windows, some with classic Spanish-style wrought-iron grillwork, and an irregular tiled roofline. In the 1920s architect Addison Mizner (1893–1933) was to refine this style for his huge mansions in Palm Beach, but in the early 1900s this architecture was unusual, particularly in the Northeast. (Of all the many houses built along the north shore of Long Island between 1890 and 1918, for instance, only one, other than those built by Mizner, was Spanish-influenced, and that was by a little-known architect, J. Clinton Mackenzie, who built it for himself.)

The interior of the house has strong Italianate design elements, such as the sixty-foot-long gallery that runs through the center of the building, with arches, marble floors, and Rococo ceilings. The main staircase has two elegantly curved banisters, as in Blairsden, with a large Palladian stained-glass window overlooking the central landing. The living room has parquet floors, a marble fireplace, and a coffered ceiling with intricate carved decoration. French doors open onto a loggia, or conservatory, with diamond-shaped gray and white marble and granite floors, and a vaulted ceiling. Perhaps the most beautiful room in the house is the library/ballroom, a twenty-seven-by-thirty-three-foot room with a herringbone patterned parquet floor, oak paneling, and an exquisitely coffered ceiling picked out in gold. The second floor has eight bedrooms, with the servants' quarters on the third floor.

The house announces its importance by means of a long, curling driveway that brings the visitor into the courtyard through two imposing square pillars topped by finials in the shape of urns. The Olmsted Brothers were brought in by Kunhardt at the very beginning of the project to design the larger landscape. "I have recently purchased about 175 acres of field and woodland near Morristown, N.J., which I shall lay out as a country-seat," Kunhardt

wrote to the Boston-based firm in a letter dated July 10, 1896. From other contemporary correspondence, it is possible to deduce that the Olmsteds collaborated on this commission with John R. Brinley, a landscape architect responsible for several properties in the Mountain Colony, and who also designed the Morristown Green in 1908. There is little left of their work today. The grounds surrounding the house are now reduced to lawns and a few fine old trees, but the view from the top of the bluff on which the house is situated—thirteen acres of rolling hills and woods—makes up for the lack of a garden.

Urn-topped columns flank the main entrance to Faircourt, which opens onto a Mediterranean-style courtyard. Wrought-iron grillwork and balustrades at the windows, uneven tiled roofs with dormers, and a front door with Corinthian pilasters and a tiled pediment are consistent with the Italianate architecture of the house.

Henry Kunhardt named his house Blythewood. After it was sold to Colonel Anthony B. Kuser in the early 1900s, the Kusers renamed it Faircourt, in honor of a house they already owned. The Kusers were a large and influential family, several of whom settled in the Somerset Hills and built impressive summer residences. Kuser's original Faircourt was a massive Greek Revival mansion with four two-story porticos, huge pediments with oculi, and balustrades. (He is said to have maintained an aviary with the finest pheasants in the world.) Colonel Kuser donated High Point State Park to the state of New Jersey and died in 1929, the year before the park opened.

The first Faircourt, like many of these turn-of-the-century "country-seats," was later demolished. The Depression and World War II made it more difficult, even for these millionaires, to maintain such large estates. However, the founding families of Peapack, Gladstone, and Bernardsville made a lasting contribution to the area by buying up huge parcels of land (largely for fox-hunting purposes) and thus protecting it from later twentieth-century development. Post, Dillon, Schley, Engelhard, Kuser, Roebling, Whitney, Pierrepont, Pyne, and Brady—names of the American ruling aristocracy for the first years of the twentieth century—all lived and played in these beautiful hills, and many descendants still remain.

After several changes of ownership, the interior of Faircourt has lost some of its glamour, but the dark elegance of the ballroom still evokes the summer dances enjoyed by the rich families of the Mountain Colony, and the conservatory still seems the perfect background for an F. Scott Fitzgerald short story, his young men and women with their voices full of money, running through the light-filled loggia to play tennis or croquet. While so many of these great houses are long gone, Faircourt and Blairsden (p. 155) are two Gilded Age monuments still standing, witnesses to perhaps the greatest period of wealth and confidence in American history.

Brady Garden

LAMINGTON, SOMERSET COUNTY

In a rural part of central New Jersey in the mid-1700s, the Mill House stood at the edge of a road that used to run between the house and the Black River (also called the Lamington River), crossing a bridge designed in the form of an A-frame, constructed with what was called "Queen's Post" beams. In the next hundred years, the Mill House became the center of a thriving agricultural community that included a saw mill, grist mill, textile mill, and the ancillary barns, cottages, chicken houses, blacksmith's shop, and other outbuildings that supplied the needs of the local inhabitants.

By the mid-1830s a Dutch settler called Richard Sutton Vliet owned the mills, plus the 134-acre farm, and the area became known as Vliettown, a name that still resonates in the memories of old-time residents. The Mill House had become a stagecoach stop by this period, and a ledger from 1843 still exists, listing names and purchases of the travelers passing through. Perhaps the area's most famous visitor in the mid-nineteenth century was Horace Greeley, founder of the *New York Tribune* and presidential candidate in 1872, who visited the Mill House on several occasions to pursue Mary Cheney, the teacher at the one-room schoolhouse near the river. He was more successful in this than in his run for the presidency, and he married her in 1836.

In 1904 the Brady family purchased five thousand acres, which were made up of many working farms, including the Mill House at Vliettown. In 1929 James and Eliot Brady, as a

FACING *The Black River flows through the bottom of the garden, planted here with pink 'Bonica'
roses and dark purple columbines, a color combination created by the artist's eye of Joan Brady.*

137

ABOVE *The Spring Garden at the west side of the house, designed by Nelva Weber, is enclosed by a "Charleston" wall. It has four concave beds planted with* Campanula poscharskayana. *In the center a little boy with a fishing rod overlooks a small diamond-shaped pool with a fountain.*
RIGHT *A light-dappled flight of stone steps, aglow with campanula and snow-in-summer, leads from the Spring Garden to the main sweep of lawn below.*

The former stagecoach stop, now used as the artist's studio, is situated next to an old A-frame bridge, constructed with original "Queen's Post" beams.

At one end of the Spring Garden, a small boy,
flanked by geraniums, stands in a niche formed
by what was once an outdoor hearth.

new bride and groom, settled into the Mill House after renovating and adding to the house and property. In 1975, succeeding his parents, Jim Brady and his wife Joan moved in and became the current residents. Over the years the original post road was closed, and some of the land was sold to various family members.

Joan Brady is a painter, and she uses the original stagecoach stop across the bridge as a studio. The interior of the house was added to during the Bradys' tenure, and the newly designed kitchen and living room pay homage to the beautiful landscape outside that has survived over two hundred fifty years of encroaching development.

The garden has an old-world feel that reflects the simple, but powerful, history of the land in which it was nurtured. Mostly designed by Joan herself, who specializes in flower-painting, the garden has plants and shrubs that are painterly in color and shape, yet seem to flow naturally from the architecture. The front terrace outside the kitchen and dining room, for example, is a symphony of pinks, blues, and whites (peonies, campanulas, snow-in-summer, roses), framing pieces of statuary (including a bronze of Nathan Hale, the Yale graduate and

martyr of the American Revolution, found in the cellar when the Bradys first moved in) that act as focal points for the blooms. The Spring Garden, to the east of the house, is more formal, enclosed by a "Charleston" wall designed by Nelva Weber. The four concave-shaped beds of this parterre, divided by brick paths that lead to a central fountain, are framed by a small sky-blue *Campanula poscharskayana*, with pink geraniums in the center.

Joan Brady furnishes a different palette for her garden with the changing seasons. As the summer progresses, the colors of the flowers become more intense. In a book she published in 1999 about the death of her mother, *Another Kind of Time*, she described the garden on Bastille Day, July 14: "The coreopsis is a bright yellow gold; platycodon, violet blue, white

From the bridge, the view of the waterfall, decorated with 'New Dawn' roses, sums up the pastoral beauty of this garden landscape.

nicotiana, cosmos. Pink, peach, white lilies; lavender-pink phlox just put in, alchemilla's acid green leaves, orange-peach daylilies . . ."

A sweep of lawn draws the eye away from these dazzling displays of color down to the river, where the serenely flowing waterfall (often the chosen fishing site and meditation spot for a blue heron) makes a rushing sound, and where a riot of 'New Dawn' roses tumbles over the unusually formed struts of the bridge. Across the bridge, a trace of the old road, now grass-covered, leads to Joan's studio, which looks out on a view of cinnamon, honey, peach, and citron-colored fields dotted with hay bales, the Black River coursing through them like a streak of sparkling ink. With its original beams and windows, this old cottage provides a brilliantly simple background for the artist's creative vision. This is the place where "to truly see in painting," as she writes in her book, "is to allow time to stand still."

This is unquestionably a painter's garden, but behind the range of colors and patterns that the Bradys have created is a recognition of the equally profound shades that envelop this historic land. "We may have adapted the house and its surroundings for our family and friends," Joan says, "but we are always aware that we are really just the current stewards of this place."

Bachman-Wilson House

MILLSTONE, SOMERSET COUNTY

Frank Lloyd Wright is one of the architectural giants of twentieth-century America. After the Beaux-Arts–influenced historicists, who practiced mostly in the northeastern part of the United States in the early part of the century (Stanford White, Charles Platt, Horace Trumbauer, H. H. Richardson, and Richard Hunt among others), had conceded to the International Style of Mies van der Rohe and Le Corbusier—Europeans who dominated modern architecture in the 1930s—Frank Lloyd Wright emerged out of the American Midwest and proposed a new kind of architecture entirely, made for the people, out of nature, in one organic movement.

Frank Lloyd Wright was born in Wisconsin in 1867. He studied at the University of Wisconsin and then went to Chicago, where he apprenticed with Adler and Sullivan, two pioneering architects of the modern era. Wright's brilliant draftsmanship was immediately apparent, but it was clear he had other plans than making beautiful renderings. In an article for the *Architectural Record* published in 1908, the young master declared his battle plan for residential architecture—to design as few rooms as possible, to allow them to flow into each other, and to be committed to simplicity. He announced that furniture should be built in as part of the original scheme. Other pronouncements followed: "Appliances and fixtures as such are undesirable. Assimilate them together with all appurtenances into the design of the structure." "Pictures deface walls oftener than they decorate them." "Decoration is

dangerous unless you understand it thoroughly." Perhaps his most significant statement was: "A building should appear to grow easily from its site and be shaped to harmonize with its surroundings if Nature is manifest there, and if not try to make it as quiet, substantial, and organic as She would have been were the opportunity Hers."

Today, most of these propositions seem hardly scandalous, but at the time almost all of them flew in the face of the prevailing wisdom (still mired in historicism), in particular his idea of open-space living rather than a series of boxy rooms, that the furniture be integrated into the design, and his insistence on the organic nature of the building in relation to its site.

The back of the house, with its forty-eight-foot terrace, ten-foot-high windows,
and second story, has almost the feeling of a Greek temple or pavilion.

He himself wasted no time in putting his ideas into effect. He set up a studio in Taliesin, Wisconsin, and after designing several private houses and buildings (including the W. E. Martin House, in Oak Park, Illinois, and the Larkin Building in Buffalo, New York), he developed the idea for the prairie house—a long, low building, like a bungalow, designed on a series of horizontal planes, seeming to grow organically from its foundations. The Robie House, built in 1908 in Chicago, was his earliest example. Fallingwater, in Pennsylvania, is perhaps his most famous.

Wright also invented the "Usonian" house, a planned development of affordable, open-plan homes for the middle classes, designed on similar blueprints with some standard details that could easily be constructed, and employing man-made materials like glass, concrete, and steel. Envisioning houses suited to the demands of an American-style democratic society, rather than borrowed from the European model, he created the word "Usonian" (almost comparable to "Utopian") as a metaphor for the Machine, which he embraced as "our normal tool." "Architects must be masters of the industrial means of their era," he declared.

Wright's principles were controversial, but many forward-thinking architects were enthralled by this spellbinding visionary, and his studio at Taliesin became a mecca for his adoring apostles and proselytizers. Some joined the Taliesin Fellowship, whose members worked on Wright's projects and helped run the studio. A series of emotional memoirs published over the years about their experiences heightened the legend of this complex, temperamental figure. Wright's personal affairs were full of drama, and his life was so long that by the end of it many of his ideas had either become mainstream or proved to be so impractical that they were considered the dreams of a madman. He died in 1959 at Taliesin West, a retreat and studio he built outside Scottsdale, Arizona, at the age of ninety-one.

Wright is most often associated with the Midwest and New York City, where he gained many commissions (the most famous being the Guggenheim Museum), so it comes as something of a surprise that he designed four houses in New Jersey, all of which still exist. Lawrence and Sharon Tarantino own one of them, not far from Princeton. (The others are in Bernardsville, Glen Ridge, and Cherry Hill.) The Tarantinos' house, which they acquired in 1988, is called the Bachman-Wilson House, after the original owners, who built it in 1954. It is a typical Usonian house, modest in size (designed originally for a family with one child), built in concrete, glass, and wood, with open-plan living areas. Atypically, it has a second-story mezzanine with two bedrooms and cantilevered balconies, thus making it structurally taller than most of Wright's Usonian residences and enhancing its strikingly graceful appearance.

The Bachman-Wilson House is an excellent example of Wright at his most inventive and unconventional. Siting the house was a challenge, for it is located right on a main street, among several historic buildings. To solve the problem, Wright proposed that the house be set back as far as possible. The curving driveway conceals the front of the house, which offers an almost blank façade to the street, ensuring privacy both inside and out. The back of the

*The open-plan living-dining-kitchen area, a favorite Wright floor plan, has a red concrete
floor and mostly original (or meticulously restored) furniture designed by the architect.*

house, with its soaring windows and cantilevered balconies, opens out to the natural land-scape that Wright always insisted be part of the architecture. The contrast of these two façades gives almost the effect of a stage set.

To further the relationship between architecture and nature, Wright designed ten-foot-high windows and French doors along the back of the house, providing fifty-four feet of continuous glass that attracts the view outside almost like a magnet, making a powerful con-nection between the house and the sweep of lawn and trees that leads down to the Millstone River. A long, stepped terrace, made of concrete, runs forty-eight feet along the back of the house, providing an elegant pavilion that bridges the interior and exterior. An interesting clerestory, made of perforated boards or plywood cutouts, designed in geometric, angular patterns, creates a decorative effect, reminiscent of a classical frieze, along the roofline.

The open-plan living room, dining area, and kitchen are characteristic expressions of Wright's idea that traffic should flow freely between spaces. The long, diagonal exposures ensure that family and friends are not closed off from each other in separate boxes. (He even designed unusually low dining chairs, so that the view to the outside from the built-in seating in the living room would be unimpeded.) Uncarpeted floors, made of red concrete, reflect light and unify the space. The layers of wood for ceilings and window treatments, along with the concrete walls scored with horizontal lines, the long banquette and built-in bookshelves against the living room wall, create a grid effect, one of Wright's favorite design techniques. Other typical Wright contributions are the radiant heat and passive solar systems, casement windows, a carport, and the use of "waylite" concrete block, glass, and Philippine mahogany throughout the house. Basements and attics are eliminated.

Lawrence Tarantino, AIA, is an architect, and his wife, Sharon, is a designer, so thanks to their professional skills and admiration for this famous architect, the house has remained a faithful representation of Wright's work. Any changes (rebuilding the kitchen, repairing the roof, and restoring furniture and finishes) have been made with meticulous reference to Wright's original plans for the house, and most of the alterations have been directed toward restoration rather than modification or the imposition of any new components. (The original carport was turned into an office by the previous owners, which the Tarantinos hope to remove one day.) The furniture, chairs, tables, bookshelves, and light fixtures are either Wright originals, frequently made from surplus materials left over from the house's construction (as suggested by the always economically minded architect) or reconstructions from Wright's plans.

This respectful approach would surely have gratified Wright. "Through living in and working on the house, we have developed expertise, and we have consulted with other people who own Wright houses," says Lawrence Tarantino. He is a member of the technical advisory committee to Wright homeowners; Sharon is a board member of the Frank Lloyd Wright Building Conservancy.

While there are, fortunately, many examples of Frank Lloyd Wright buildings still in good condition in various parts of the country, this simple, linear house stands out, not only because of its architecture, but also because of its symbolism as a model of the middle-class housing that Wright dreamed would transform the face of suburban America. It seems appropriate that New Jersey, the most populous state for its size in the nation, should be a beneficiary of his idiosyncratic genius.

Blairsden

PEAPACK, SOMERSET COUNTY

By the late nineteenth century, the newly prosperous titans of industry had built their great mansions along Fifth Avenue in New York, each one bigger and grander than its neighbor, as architects made obeisance to their clients' success in banking, mining, or the railroads, stuffing each one with more and more paintings and furniture as their interior decorators urged upon them the exportable treasures of Europe. It was now time for these millionaire businessmen to move out of the city, to create country estates that would mirror their urban status, and give their families a place in the summertime to relax, play tennis, and enjoy the garden, those pleasures that the world's aristocracies had so conspicuously luxuriated in for centuries.

Some went north to the Hudson Valley. Some looked east to Long Island. Others decided that the most desirable location for building a country house was in the state of New Jersey. As the Erie-Lackawanna railway line reached Bernardsville, and then on to Peapack and Gladstone, the glorious scenery of the Somerset Hills, only fifty miles from New York City, was revealed to real estate speculators' hungry eyes. Could there be a more ideal place for a country estate than nestled within these blue hills, with the Raritan River sparkling in the summer breezes, and evergreen forests stretching as far as the eye could see?

C. Ledyard Blair certainly thought not, and in 1897 he and his wife bought the Mellick Farm, a 423-acre property in Peapack. The farm had recently been immortalized by Andrew

FACING *The three-hundred-foot-long ornamental pool in front of this classic Gilded Age mansion reflects the imposing entrance of the house, dominated by an ornate limestone front door. Billy Prouty Photography © 1996.*

ABOVE *This finely sculpted Italian marble ram, garlanded with fruits, is one of a
pair acting as "bookends" for a bench overlooking the main terrace of Blairsden.*
FACING *This bust of a Roman emperor is one of twelve flanking the reflecting pool in front of the
main entrance of Blairsden. They were purchased from the French government in the 1890s.*

D. Mellick, Jr., in his book, originally titled *The Story of an Old Farm*, a rambling, but vivid,
history of his farm and the German families who founded the Peapack and Bedminster communities in the prerevolutionary period. The book was first published in 1889 and garnered
considerable praise for the author's impressive research, storytelling, and understanding of
human nature. Whether C. Ledyard Blair knew about or read the book is doubtful. He was
surely less interested in the history of the place than in the dream of creating a magnificent
country seat that would reflect his cultural sophistication and social position in the world.

Ledyard Blair was the scion of a prominent New Jersey family. His grandfather was John

The south façade of the house, designed by Carrère & Hastings, dramatically reveals its French-style architecture, with its immense terraces, steeply pitched multilevel slate roofline, tall chimneys, dormers, and quoined detailing. Billy Prouty Photography © 1996.

Insley Blair, who was born in 1802, at the beginning of the explosive century that was to make him, and many others, millionaires. Blair's start was with a general store in a town later named Blairstown. He began making his millions in the coal business in Pennsylvania, and he finally became president of sixteen railroads. By the mid-nineteenth century he was known as "The Railroad King of the West." His son, Dewitt Clinton (named after the governor of New York), went into the family business and founded Blair Academy in New Jersey. Clinton Ledyard Blair was born in 1867. He graduated from Princeton University in 1890 and created, with his father and grandfather, the financial firm Blair and Company, on Wall Street, which became very successful, particularly as bankers for the ever-expanding railroad consortiums.

Blair's decision to buy land in the Somerset Hills was regarded by many of his friends as a risky gesture. Although the land was very close to the city, at this time the railroad only went as far as Bernardsville, and since automobiles were not yet in common use, access was not easy. But Blair was confident about his pioneering move, knowing he had found one of the most beautiful locations in the area for his house—high on a mountaintop, overlooking the unspoiled New Jersey hills and the river below.

Having selected the site, Blair made his next most important decision, his choice of architect. He commissioned the firm of Carrère & Hastings, the distinguished New York architects who were the recipients of one of the city's most significant assignments, the design of the New York Public Library, which was completed in 1911. John Carrère and Thomas Hastings had apprenticed with the city's most successful firm, McKim, Mead & White, before starting out on their own. Steeped in the teaching of the Beaux-Arts School in Paris, which was devoted to the classical principles of architecture, they were associated with buildings influenced largely by the European traditions and dedicated, like most of the competing firms of the period, to a form of exuberant historicism.

For such an imposing client, Carrère & Hastings designed a three-story Louis XIII chateau, made of rose-colored brick and creamy limestone, with dormers, pediments, balustrades, columns, quoins, and a steeply pitched slate roof. The house was constructed with steel beams and reinforced concrete, with thirty-inch-thick walls, solid enough to withstand any weather to which this New Jersey mountaintop might be exposed. The interior is equally extravagant. Blairsden has thirty-eight rooms and twenty-five fireplaces, decorated with imported marble and tile, bronze and brass, crystal chandeliers, elaborate plasterwork, glazed tile flooring, and exquisite woodwork in walnut, oak, olive, and mahogany. The main staircase has a fine curving double banister that echoes the one in Rosecliff, Newport, designed by Stanford White for Mrs. Hermann Oelrichs. Blairsden has a two-story kitchen with a balcony, a baking room, a walnut-paneled library, and a billiard room with walls covered in hand-tooled Moroccan leather. The house was begun in 1898 and completed in 1902. The price was two million dollars, which in today's value is approximately twenty-five million dollars.

To build this extraordinary piece of architecture on top of a steep hill was in itself a formidable challenge. The land had to be leveled and terraced (in an age before the invention of bulldozers). A funicular railway with a wood-burning fire was built to bring materials and workers up to the site. Masons, carpenters, plasterers, and painters poured in from all over the country to produce the astonishing interior detailing specified by the architects. Many of the more skilled craftsmen were procured from Italy, just as they were for the building of Biltmore, George Vanderbilt's mansion in Asheville, North Carolina. (In both cases, some of the Italian families stayed on, becoming permanent residents of the community.)

But the house was only one element of Carrère & Hastings's vision for Blairsden. Thomas Hastings in particular was an enthusiast of formal gardens, as can be seen in his design for Bryant Park, which was based on the Luxembourg Gardens in Paris. The architects hired James Leal Greenleaf (1857–1933), designer of the Lincoln Memorial, to create a fitting garden for their magnificent chateau. Greenleaf designed two large terraces on the south side of the chateau, which look out onto the unparalleled view of the lake (which Blair had made by damming the river), forests, and hills. These terraces are bisected by a wide stone staircase leading down from the patio outside the living room. At the far corner of each terrace,

The view from the main terrace, down a series of cascades and canals where water once flowed, offers a breathtaking view of the hills and trees of central New Jersey, as unspoiled as they were over one hundred years ago.

a smaller staircase goes down to a lower level, with arches and a balustrade forming the architecture of its northern wall, a design idea frequently seen in the Baroque gardens of Italy, such as Villa Garzoni in Tuscany. At each end of this terrace, a narrow staircase leads down to yet another level, with a fountain at its center. From this level, a double waterfall— another Baroque feature—cascades down four hundred feet to the lake below.

The main entrance, dominated by an ornate limestone front door, with massive pediments and columns, is on the west side of the house. It overlooks a three-hundred-foot formal canal, lined with maples and rows of busts of Roman emperors on pedestals, acquired by Ledyard Blair from the French government. Originally there were swans swimming in the water. The maples were planted full-grown, having been dragged up the hill to their destination by teams of horses. Blair's penchant for moving fully grown trees and shrubs became legendary among the locals. "On Sunday a number of heavy wagons loaded with boxwood trees passed through Main Street," reported a contemporary account of Blair's amazing earthworks. "Wagons similarly loaded have passed through town nearly every day during the past month and have excited the curiosity of a number of townspeople. Each wagon contains one diminutive tree set in a great box filled with earth that makes a heavy load for one team."

The report goes on to say, "Mr. Blair's latest investment in boxwood trees exceeds his great expenditure last winter when he moved one hundred mammoth trees by wagon ten miles over mountain roads and transplanted them about his new residence." It was added that boxwood was the rarest tree found in New Jersey, and that they were frequently moved from the lawns of private residences "where the owners have been induced to part with them for a generous price." (Today mature palm trees suffer a similar fate as they are acquired for the gardens of the wealthy in Palm Beach and Boca Raton.) What the report politely omitted to mention was that several wooden bridges in the county broke under the weight of these huge, balled-up trees, and that Blair had to replace them.

The boxwood is long gone, and the fountains are dry, but it is clear that the gardens of Blairsden were stunning, even in an era of great gardens. Dogwoods, eastern red cedars, wisterias, forsythia, magnolia, and an avenue of lindens still survive as memorials to that great Italianate masterpiece created over a hundred years ago.

Ledyard Blair and his family enjoyed Blairsden for forty-seven years, with a staff of twenty-two indoor servants and fifty gardeners. Blair died in 1949, and in 1950 the 423-acre estate was broken up. The house, plus approximately thirty acres, was sold by the family at auction to the Sisters of St. John the Baptist for $65,000. Most of the interior furniture and furnishings remained just as the Blairs had left them. While the price seems laughable, it must be remembered that after World War II, residential real estate was in the doldrums, and nobody wanted a huge, unmanageable French chateau that was in serious need of repair plus a staff of over twenty to run it.

The nuns were deeply respectful of the house they renamed "St. Joseph's Villa," and they attempted to keep as much of the interior intact as possible. They turned the ballroom into Our Lady's Chapel and used the house as a retreat for over forty-six years, before finally giving up the task of maintaining such a vast enterprise and putting it back on the market.

Today, Blairsden may have lost some of its extravagant air, and the gardens their verdant and watery elegance, but its architecture is still a triumph, and the interior still displays some of the finest craftsmanship of the period. "This is a major, major architectural work in the state," says Mark Alan Hewitt, author of *The Architect & the American Country House*. "It needs to be taken care of and stewarded into the future."

Slack Garden

PEAPACK, SOMERSET COUNTY

Although the first wave of country-house building in the Oldwick-Peapack-Bernardsville area took place in the late 1890s, this beautifully unspoiled part of New Jersey continued to attract escapees from the city into the mid-twentieth century. In the late 1920s the architect Musgrove Hyde, of Hyde & Shepard of New York, designed a large house in the French style for Frank Johnson. Called Ellistan, the house is built of unusual soft brownstone, and the roof is made of Lucerne tile. With its steeply pitched rooflines, dormers, and tall chimneys, the house makes an imposing impression as it rises up at the end of the driveway.

The house is now owned by Mr. and Mrs. Hank Slack, who live here with their six children. Mr. Slack is a grandson of Roger Mellick, a Wall Street stockbroker who once owned a house in nearby Far Hills called Middlebrook, also designed by Musgrove Hyde and built at about the same time as Ellistan. (Hyde was a popular local architect; he also designed a house for the Scribner family in Far Hills in the 1920s.)

The front façade of Ellistan faces north over the pastures and hills of New Jersey's hunting country. Originally, the gardens of Ellistan consisted mostly of trees, shrubs, a small pond, and a paddock, on a property that now amounts to approximately eighty acres. When the house was purchased in 1985, significant landscaping was carried out by George Betsill, but it was only in 1991 that Hank Slack's cousin Shelby Mellick created the fundamental

FACING *Ellistan shows off its impressive stature, with its steeply pitched roof and tall chimneys, at the end of a long, winding driveway.*

ABOVE *A cascade of pink 'Eden' roses dances in wild abandon on a trellis in the garden-patio on the south side of the house.*
FACING *The formal entrance to the sunken garden opens onto a circular lawn, framed by flower borders, with a pond as the focal point. The garden, situated on the east side of the house, was originally created by Shelby Mellick.*

RIGHT *English garden designer Penelope Hobhouse transformed this corner of the formal garden into a seating area, with a flagstone patio and a formal arrangement of containers. The yew hedge at the back is trimmed low so the glorious view over the fields is exposed.*

BELOW *A blue heron serenely spouts water into the lily pond, while arches of climbing roses in the background soften the austere contours of the house.*

FACING *One of a pair of iron greyhounds stands guard over the lavish expanse of central New Jersey's hills and farmlands, where no trace of intrusive civilization interrupts the pastoral vista.*

blueprint of the gardens as they are today. "She has a wonderful eye and great taste," says Sarah Slack.

It was her inspiration to create a formal garden on the east side of the house, using the pond as the focal point of the square plan. The blue heron in the center of the pond came from New Hope, Pennsylvania. She designed iron arches on the south side, over which she grew roses, and established large flower beds within the square format. She also had the idea to create a white garden to the south of the house, surrounding the patio that had been designed by George Betsill. In order to achieve this, she removed two large holly trees that seemed to accentuate the imposing feeling of the architecture, and she added a trellis around the garden and patio, over which the rose 'Eden' grows in wild abundance in summer, giving the impression of airiness, and at the same time offering privacy.

After Hank Slack married Sarah, Shelby insisted on handing the gardens over to her. "I knew nothing about gardens," Sarah confesses, "but I felt that they needed an even stronger sense of design, particularly surrounding such a dominating house. I wanted to get a feeling of containment and privacy—a sense of coziness. The house is masculine and somewhat austere."

Sarah, who is English, and her husband had both lived in London, and they knew the work of Penelope Hobhouse, the English garden designer. They also had friends in common. Sarah contacted Penelope in England to ask if she would have a look at the garden on one of her trips to America. Soon after, the distinguished gardener arrived at the house. According to Sarah, "She came very late one night, and by breakfast the following morning she had already spent time in the gardens and made numerous drawings."

Penelope Hobhouse has been designing gardens all over the world for more than thirty years. Until 1993 she and her husband, John Malins, were in charge of the National Trust Gardens at Tintinhull House in Somerset, one of the most visited gardens in England. Some of her distinguished designs include a garden for the late Queen Mother at Walmer Castle, in Kent, the "Country Garden" for the Royal Horticultural Society at Wisley, outside London, and an herb garden for the New York Botanical Garden.

Her style is eclectic, but like most English gardeners, she believes in strong architectural shapes and axes, large, deeply planted borders, a soft color palette, and an overall balance between art and nature. While she has a deep understanding of horticulture, perhaps Penelope Hobhouse's most important contribution to gardening is her practicality. She has a no-nonsense approach. "Often the garden has to fulfill a twofold purpose," she writes briskly. "To satisfy an overall aesthetic need, which will include some link with the architecture of the house; and to be a place where plants are grown successfully." Nothing could be clearer than that.

For Ellistan, Penelope Hobhouse's mission was specific—to create garden rooms that incorporated the landscape in which the house is situated. To this end, she planted a yew hedge along the northern perimeter of the formal garden, thus enclosing the space, yet encompassing the view stretching out beyond it. She added a hornbeam hedge at the south end to create a further sense of enclosure. She enlarged the beds, but she placed a path through them, which simultaneously divides the spaces and enables one to walk in the garden, not just view it from a distance. She also balanced the iron arches that Shelby Mellick had designed with further arches on the north side. These have been planted with roses and clematis that intertwine and will eventually create a tunnel effect.

In order to make both the formal garden and the white garden link together, she extended the existing hemlock hedge to the south, which has resulted in uniting the gardens and creating an additional "room." Penelope also encouraged Sarah and Hank to sink the children's trampoline into the ground, for both safety and aesthetic reasons, and to plant up the bank around it with more shrubs, including *Rosa rugosa* and viburnum, thus softening the look of this southern stretch of the garden. Nine oak trees, in three groups of three, were planted in the long, sloping lawn that leads down from the patio to the driveway and the road, in order to break up the space and add interest to this part of the landscape.

As a result of these design changes, the gardens now flow into each other, fanning out from the sides of the house in an endlessly unfolding vista, reducing the dominant nature of the architecture and allowing the space around it to breathe. "There are always glimpses of things beyond," Sarah Slack observes.

Perhaps the most astonishing aspect of this transformation is that it took place only three years ago. Looking at it now, the visitor would assume these lovely gardens had been here forever, fitting partners to the uncompromising stone house to which they are allied. Sarah Slack attributes this entirely to Gerth van Wyck, the Slacks' gardener: "Penelope left us with a wonderful design, but it is Gerth who battles daily with the effects of drought and humidity, rabbits and bugs, and, dare I say it, our numerous dogs. He never loses hope or his sense of humor and we have enormous fun watching the garden develop and occasionally daring to change the plantings." They also give credit to their English consultant. "We both learned an enormous amount from watching Penny work," says Sarah, "and I think that the house is now more comfortable in its setting."

A Private Garden

SUSSEX COUNTY

Sussex County is at the northernmost tip of the state of New Jersey, with Pennsylvania running along its western edge, and New York to the east. Sussex County is perhaps the most undeveloped part of New Jersey, with no major towns, no arterial roadways (except Route 80 that traverses its southern borders), and no vast military/industrial complex to disturb the cows, the sheep, the streams, and the woods that occupy this 521-square-mile area of bucolic countryside.

In this pastoral landscape is a forty-acre garden that has been lovingly tended and extended for nearly twenty years. The house to which it is attached is a typical Sussex County farmhouse, dated around 1850, with a barn built a few years later. The farm was abandoned in the 1940s, but in the 1950s and 1960s two families purchased it and restored it to health. The current owners bought it in 1967. They quickly set to work to make it habitable as a summer home. They put in new plumbing and electricity. They added a great room and master bedroom in a new addition. In the early 1990s another addition was made to accommodate an office and a greenhouse. It is connected to the main house by a breezeway.

Today, the place is unrecognizable. The forty acres of untamed land attached to the house have been transformed into a series of gardens and landscapes that stretch out to the horizon. The house is situated on the top of a high elevation. (All the hills that dominate this property are natural, and full of geological history.) Up an incline on the north side of the

FACING *The huge sweep of hillside garden to the northeast of the house is a mass of flowers that change with the seasons—here a summer display of delphiniums, cleome, malva, and nicotiana—contained by a low wall of rocks found on or near the property.*

In late summer, the gazebo that nestles near the border of the woods is covered in a riotous snowfall of Clematis maximowicziana.

The well-house garden (named for its original structure) is planted with handsome, pale pink tree peonies.

ABOVE *The "ruin," or folly, is an eye-catching structural feature. Newly installed with stones rescued from a barn, it consists of a series of Romanesque arches situated at the foot of a man-made stream flowing behind them from a natural rock formation.*
FACING *This serene stretch of water sits at the foot of some forty acres of garden and landscape. The pond is fed by springs. A man-made waterfall, tumbling sixty feet out of the forest, recirculates water from the pond.*

house, above an elaborately planted hillside, are a stretch of lawn, a gazebo, and a tennis court. Behind them, dense woods define the northern perimeter of the property. The front façade faces a small formal garden with a small boxwood hedge, perennials, and herbs.

To the right of the front of the house, the owners are constructing a "ruin," or folly, to create an ornamental feature on the dramatic ridge to the north of the driveway. The lovely gray stones for this ruin come from the old barn, which burned down in the late 1940s. All that remained was one stone wall about eighty feet long, which has found a dynamic new role in the architecture of the ruin, along with other stones rescued from an old railroad bridge. In building this structure, designed like a partially tumbledown wall with Romanesque arches, the owners discovered a spectacular rock formation, which is now being incorporated into a rock garden and water feature beneath the arches.

The main sweep of the garden, developed by the owners, is to the rear of the house, which faces south over a valley with woods beyond. Nearest the house, as in the great eighteenth-century European estates, is the most formal area of the garden—three to four acres of carefully planted beds and borders. Perennials are planted in the breezeway, connecting the

ABOVE *A stone staircase climbs up the hillside to the northern end of the garden, decorated with seasonal flowers and shrubs.*
RIGHT *This is a typical planting in this carefully structured garden. White* Cerastium tomentosum *foams out beneath a dark red barberry bush in a brilliant contrast of color and texture.*

A resting-place offers shade on a deck outside the back of the house, overlooking part of the expansive lawn-and-flower slope down to the lake below.

house to the office/greenhouse addition. A formal garden with perennials and herbs enclosed in boxwood is laid out in front of the house's entryway. A poolhouse terrace, a wellhouse garden, and a hillside garden also decorate this "domestic" part of the design.

The garden then unfolds out into the landscape, with trees, shrubs, and pathways. Lavender beds underplant a small orchard with apple, peach, pear, and cherry trees, with a nursery garden and vegetable garden below. A shed and greenhouse nurture young plants. At the far end of this rich panoply of colors, scents, and shapes is a lake, with an artificial waterfall tumbling sixty feet out of the forest down a dramatic bank of rocks. While both husband and wife are deeply involved in the development of the property, he has entrusted the design of the garden to his wife, who designed the waterfall, as well as creating and executing the whole concept of this complex scenery.

The work is ongoing and phenomenally demanding. A deer fence had to be installed around the whole perimeter of the property. The ground is unforgiving—rock, clay, and hardpan. In the garden by the gazebo there was sand down to fifteen feet. Enormous amounts of compost (peat moss and horse manure) had to be brought in. "One year for Mother's Day

LEFT *Behind the shed, the nursery garden is like a holding pen for a large number of plants, which are nurtured and experimented with. Here columbine, variegated brunnera, armeria, coral bells, and pansy ('Bowles Black') await their turn for promotion.* **BELOW** *Another striking combination of plants creates texture and subtle color contrasts—*Sedum *'Indian Chief,'* Pennisetum alopecuroides, *and* Calamagrostis acutiflora stricta.

TOP LEFT *The interior of the gazebo has an amusing collection of wooden tennis rackets on the ceiling— a mark of the owners' sporting interest.*
TOP RIGHT *Outside the front of the house is a small formal garden and archway, framed in a white climbing* Hydrangea petiolaris, *opening to a pond with a fountain and a small bronze nymph from Belgium.*
BOTTOM LEFT *The greenhouse contains a dazzling display of tender plants, including orchids, ferns, and mandevilla. These are brought into the garden in the summertime.*
BOTTOM RIGHT *At the lower end of the garden, an orchard with fruit trees such as apple, peach, pear, and cherry are underplanted with lavender.*

RIGHT *One of the many specimen plants that decorate this garden— a purple clematis 'Elsa Spaeth.'*
BELOW *Flowers are not the only important elements of the garden. This frog is master of the universe as it surveys the glorious landscape it inhabits.*

my sons gave me a truckload of horse manure," confesses the garden designer. "I was very happy." She had to analyze the soil and test it constantly, to find out what would grow. "Although people think that the East Coast generally provides an acid-loving soil, here in this part of Sussex County we are on a limestone ridge, with a high pH factor," she explains. "There are no oak trees, azaleas, or rhododendrons. Blueberries and mountain laurel also hate the soil here. But instead we can grow hellebores, clematis, and daphne with great success."

All the gardening is organic—no chemicals or poisons of any kind. "We prove it can be done," she says. "I feel very strongly about it." In the greenhouse she introduces frogs and lizards that sustain the balance of the microcosm. "They keep down aphids. We also import ladybugs," she says. "They are all very effective."

She was helped along the way by a landscape architect, but much of the design of this huge garden is hers. It is difficult to control a landscape on such a large scale, but the definitions of each planted area are very clear, thanks to the careful placement of stones, steps, paths, and ground cover. Most of the stonework for the hillsides is local limestone. To give focus or to pull together a bed or hillside, she likes to mass the same plant, such as mounds of white cerastium or a field of lavender. She experiments with colors—black violas, pale peach-colored tree peonies, and purple clematis. The "ruin" on the north side of the house is being planted in a totally red palette, consisting of peonies, phlox, lupines, scabiosa, verbena, a young hawthorn tree called "Crimson Cloud"—"and some really wild three-foot-tall Jack-in-the-pulpits." Red-leafed caladiums fill in the blank spots in the shaded areas.

With all this attention to detail, she is relaxed about her plants' performance. "I have a tendency to let them do what they want to do," she says. Her greatest expertise is in plant knowledge, acquired through study and by visiting a lot of gardens abroad, particularly in England. She knows the names and species of countless plants, many of which she experiments with here at home. She has also been helped over the years by two water garden and rock specialists, and she has a gifted manager who oversees the planting and maintenance of the garden.

While the property was originally just a summer home, now the owners live here all year round. With such a garden to come home to, who can blame them?

Abraham Van Campen House

COLUMBIA, WARREN COUNTY

Six miles north of the Delaware Water Gap is a long, low-slung farmhouse, situated on a bluff above Old Mine Road in Warren County. Sheltered by honey locust, hackberry, and cherry trees, it is hardly visible from the road. When examined more closely, it seems to look out over the small beaver pond beneath it (formerly a marsh) with little awareness of the great weight it carries of the history, not only of the state of New Jersey, but also of the origins of the New World itself.

The house was built between 1725 and 1732 by Abraham Van Campen, a member of the large Van Campen family who settled here with many other Dutch immigrants in the early eighteenth century, drawn by the potential of this wild, mountainous region. Although the history is cloudy, it is believed that Van Campen built the house over the period of about a year. He returned to his former home in Esopus, New York (now Kingston), to marry, and the newlyweds then moved into the newly finished farmhouse. Here the family prospered, owning vast tracts of land, plus a sawmill, grist mill, and other businesses that sprouted up along the strategically important Old Mine Road.

Old Mine Road is one of the most historic highways in the country. Said to be the first road of any length built in the United States, it dates from as early as 1632, when it was known as the King's Highway. Later the Queen's Highway, in 1682 it was called "the Path of the

FACING *This charming prerevolutionary farmhouse on Old Mine Road, overlooking the Delaware Water Gap, is a unique architectural gem. It looks more like a West Country cottage in England than a prosperous family home built by Dutch immigrants between 1725 and 1732.*

Great Valley," thanks to its winding route along the Delaware River, the Kittatinny Mountains rising in dramatic formations on either side of the roaring current of the river.

The Minisink Indians took this 104-mile trail from Big Minisink Island, where their ancient dwellings and burial grounds were, down south to Pahaquarry (derived from the Lenni Lenape name for "a place between the mountains beside the waters") in Warren County and as far north as Kingston, New York. The importance of the road became apparent to outsiders when copper and other minerals were discovered in the valley, and soon various explorers, including the West Indian Company and pioneer miners from Holland, made their way to Old Mine Road and built houses along its borders. Churches and ferries soon dotted the landscape, as the largely Dutch population expanded in response to the almost unlimited promise of the land. (The rich alluvial soil of the valley supported record crops for both buckwheat and corn during the last two centuries.)

Although initially there was harmony between the new settlers and the Indians, by the mid-eighteenth century the atmosphere became increasingly hostile, largely initiated by a fraud perpetrated on the Indians by agents of William Penn. Penn had come to the area and arranged a treaty with the Minisink tribe whereby Penn would obtain ownership of all the land between the Delaware River and the number of miles northwards that a man could walk in three days. Penn himself set off on the walk north with the Indians in an atmosphere of great affability, until Penn, after a day and a half, decided he had walked far enough. The party agreed to make the land deal where he stood, and a monument was erected to mark the spot. But Penn's successors decided to renege and demanded a further walk that would give them more land. Ultimately they claimed ownership of another eighty-six miles, which the Indians declared had been acquired through trickery. This finagling on the part of the white men, sadly typical of many broken deals with the Indians throughout the New World, left the Minisinks hurt and angry, and bent on reprisal.

Between 1755 and 1758 Old Mine Road was the scene of many bloody massacres, and vivid descriptions remain of the fierce fighting that took place along the trail during these three years of strife. The Van Campen family often found themselves in life-threatening situations with stories of scalpings, tomahawkings, and other acts of violence spreading like wildfire between the houses along the well-known trail. In 1758 the governors of New Jersey and Pennsylvania met with the Indians and negotiated a peace, the Indians settling for one thousand pounds and abandoning all claims on the New Jersey territory (a settlement that was to cost the winning negotiators dearly).

With calm restored, Abraham Van Campen and his family increased their dominance in the community, becoming justices of the peace and playing a major role in the development of the region. But peace was again interrupted by the French and Indian War, which reached as far inland as the Delaware Water Gap, and once again the local settlers were threatened by Indian raids. (The peace negotiated in 1758 had not eradicated the sense of wrong lingering in the minds of many of the Minisink tribe.) Nine Hessian soldiers were bivouacked

FACING *The house is masonry over fieldstone, with two- to three-foot-thick walls. The original wooden porch has gone, and the dormers are Victorian, but the simple features of this sturdy landmark retain the atmosphere of a rural retreat built over three hundred years ago.*

Much painful history has passed through this house, which has endured wars with the Minisink Indians, the French and Indian War, and the Revolutionary War. The house also served as a stockade, a stagecoach stop, and a post office, before coming to rest under the present owner.

at Abraham Van Campen's farmhouse, as well as mercenaries involved in the war, so it is probable that the house was stockaded and used as a fortress during this period. The American Revolution continued to create a serious threat to the Van Campens and their neighbors. The river became the site of several massacres as the Indians joined forces with the Tories, and in 1778 the Battle of Minisink, the largest battle in the history of the Old Mine Road, produced atrocities on such a scale that the American soldiers retreated en masse.

By the nineteenth century, the Old Mine Road region was restored to serenity. Abraham Van Campen, who had served in both wars, becoming a militia colonel during the French and Indian War, died in 1806 and is buried in the Presbyterian Cemetery in Shawnee, Pennsylvania. His sons, Abraham and Moses, who lived in the house, also took part in the two devastating wars that scarred the region. The house later became a stagecoach stop and post office, and it has been inhabited almost continually until the present day. Jean Zipser, who lives here now, comes from a family who has lived in the valley since 1926 and has owned the house since 1932. As founder of the Pahaquarry Foundation, a nonprofit institution supporting local artists, writers, and students in the fields of art and history, Ms. Zipser is thoroughly versed in the historical and political lore of the region. The fact that she lives in and loves one of the most significant buildings on Old Mine Road seems delightfully appropriate.

"The house is masonry over fieldstone," she explains, "and the walls are between two and three feet thick. An original floor plan of the house shows it measuring twenty-six by fifty-two feet—very modest. There have been some changes made. The dormers are Victorian, probably 1800s, and the original wooden porch is gone."

The changes are minor compared to its overall visual consistency. The house stands on its own, charming, uncomplicated, unique, without any familiar antecedents. Its architecture does not compare to anything we think of as an American house, even a prerevolutionary or colonial one that would be of the same period. Although built by Dutch immigrants, it exhibits none of the stylistic details that we identify as belonging to Dutch Colonial architecture (no gambrel roof or flared eaves, for instance). The Abraham Van Campen House is more like a West Country cottage in England or Wales, its extraordinary history concealed forever within its soft stone walls, modest windows, and long roofline. A few miles from the seventy-thousand-acre Delaware Water Gap National Recreation Area (the largest recreation area in the eastern United States), today the Abraham Van Campen House reflects only the peacefulness of rural lives well lived, a fitting testament to the spectacular mountain and water landscape that surrounds it. ✎

Finesville

WARREN COUNTY

Few people seriously entertain the possibility that New Jersey is a rural state, yet its north-western borders, bounded by the Delaware River between Pohatcong in the south and Mata-moris north of the Water Gap, offer some of the most natural mountain and water landscapes and charming old-world villages that any escapee from urban angst could desire. One of the most appealing areas is the Musconetcong River Valley, which winds through this part of the country from Riegelsville in Pennsylvania through Finesville, Warren Glen, Blooms-bury, and on into the central part of Warren County, New Jersey. Wildlife management ar-eas, trout hatcheries, game farms, covered bridges, grasslands, and natural forests are all part of the spectacular scenery along the banks of this river. While the noisy Hudson and Del-aware may have imprinted themselves on the map as the major waterways of the Northeast, the lovely Musconetcong sparkles modestly in the small print, protected by its long, green valleys and surrounding woods.

Probably because of this benign neglect, the Musconetcong Valley remains rich in pre-historic relics and ancient history. One of two highly important Paleo-Indian archeological sites in New Jersey, Plenge, Warren County, produced evidence of human habitation traced back twelve thousand years. After the Wisconsin Glacier melted, bringing water into the valley, forests grew quickly, and the area was discovered by the Lenni Lenape Indians, who settled here, making trails and planting crops. As in the Delaware Water Gap region, the

FACING *This beautiful stone mill was built by the Fines, one of the most important families in the region, who came here from Germany in the mid-eighteenth century. It was a thriving wool manufactory until around 1866 and is now a private home.*

The soft local limestone with which the mill and its neighbors
are constructed is typical of the Pohatcong region.

eighteenth-century European pioneers soon recognized the Musconetcong Valley's fertility, and they not only farmed it successfully, but also created an iron industry, burning the dense forests for charcoal to fuel the furnaces. When the iron industry declined, many people left the valley, and the area reverted to its earlier natural beauty.

The industrial period left its mark, however. One of the towns with the most powerful sense of the past is Finesville, nestling at the southernmost tip of the river where it runs into the Delaware. At this point a covered toll bridge once connected Riegelsville, Bucks County, Pennsylvania, with Riegelsville, Warren County, New Jersey. The original bridge, built in 1835, was swept away by flooding in 1903, and it was replaced by the elegant suspension bridge that joins the two towns (and states) today.

Finesville was originally called Chelsea Forge, a settlement founded in 1761 in response to the iron-making that had by this time become a become a major business in the Musconetcong Valley. The Fine family (originally Fein) arrived here from Germany and in 1767 bought the forge and a two-story stone home in the town. The patriarch, Philip Fine, built on the land an oil mill, a grist mill, and a sawmill. His sons expanded their empire with a store, a wool mill, and a blacksmith's shop. These diversifications proved remarkably prescient, for by the 1800s the iron business was failing, owing to the destruction of the hardwood forests that provided the charcoal, and the mills became far more profitable.

According to local residents Dan and Pauline Campanelli, the Fines' grist mill burned down but was later rebuilt by the Riegels, another important family who gave their name to the Warren County town that was originally known as Hunt's Ferry, named for Edward Hunt, who settled here before the Revolution. Hunt was a strong supporter of the continental army, and he welcomed sixty cavalry to the town in 1778. (The Campanellis currently live in the George Hunt House, another handsome stone house, with a clapboard addition, dating circa 1825.) The Riegels, like the Fines, went into the mill business. They converted their grist mill into a sawmill, then a paper mill, which remained operational until 1980. The Riegels also owned a store and post office housed in a modest brick building in Finesville that still stands today.

The lower corner of the right façade reveals an arch that was probably part of the original watercourse from the river to the mill wheel.

One other local family deserves mention: in 1793 Benjamin Seigle bought land east of Finesville. While copying his neighbors' grist mills and blacksmith shops, he also started making pottery using a red clay from Pennsylvania. His products became well known as Seigleware. (His son, Jacob, became famous for his "redware," as it was called, and pieces can be seen today in various state museums. Jacob's son, William, continued the pottery business.) Benjamin Seigle, like his neighbors, acquired that ultimate status symbol and had a town named after him, Seigletown. This tightly knit group of German immigrant families conscientiously plied their trades in Finesville, and between the mid-eighteenth and mid-nineteenth centuries, they built a series of houses and mill buildings that remain in excellent condition today.

The most fascinating feature of Finesville is its architectural uniformity. A large number of the houses built by these families were constructed out of limestone, and thus they have survived intact, offering a vivid picture of how the town looked three hundred years ago. Even the most modern industry in Finesville, Alba Vineyard, conducts its small, but high-quality, winemaking business out of a handsome limestone dairy barn, circa 1830, that the owners have converted. The custom of construction was to use a mixture of limestone and fieldstone, with the sides and back of the house built of fieldstone, and more carefully cut limestone for the façades. These houses and barns have a decorative, yet informal, quality that is similar to the better-known stone farmhouses found in Bucks County, Pennsylvania. Their beauty resides in their simplicity and in the subtle colors and patterns of the stone.

The illustrious Fine family built this stone mill sometime around 1810 and turned it into a wool factory. Prior to the American Revolution, the British would not allow their American colonists to manufacture wool, forcing them to import the material from Britain, thus sustaining the home industry. However, after the War of 1812, this law was abolished, and the Fines were able to turn their wool manufactory into a thriving business that ran successfully until 1866.

In the 1870s, the mill was purchased by the Taylor Stiles Company and turned into a knife-rolling mill. After several other transformations, it was converted into a residence in the 1970s and is now used by the present owner, Amy Hollander, as a jewelry studio and living quarters.

She has delved deeply into the building's history. She discovered through studying old photographs that another structure originally extended from the front of the house—a timber-frame building used as a blacksmith and wheelwright shop until it was torn down in the early part of the twentieth century. Hollander says, "The first floor houses the only industrial element left of the original mill works—a truncated gear shaft which hangs from the ceiling of the studio. . . . Cornerstones revealed in the exposed stone wall of the stairwell to the second floor show evidence of an earlier one-story structure which predated the timber-frame structure, and most likely the mill as well."

On the second floor, the stone walls, ceiling joists, and deep windows are the only visible characteristics original to the design of the mill. The third floor reflects another period in its history. "From 1919 to 1951," Amy Hollander explains, "it was owned and used as a lodge for the Improved Order of the Red Men, America's oldest fraternal organization chartered by Congress." The organization was founded in 1765 as a secret society working against British rule, and its original members were responsible for the famous Boston Tea Party in 1773.

Another clue about its past is the stone arch that appears just above the ground on the right façade of the mill, under which water once flowed from the race to the wheel that worked the mill. Probably in the early twentieth century, the mill race was filled in, and this archeological relic is all that remains.

Like most of Finesville's residents, Amy Hollander deeply appreciates the treasure of which she is caretaker, and she immediately embarked upon the mission of restoring the mill to its original state. Part of the task involved removing layers of modern plaster on the exterior, revealing the beautiful stone façade, most of which had to be repointed. She hopes to replace the roof with period shingles and restore the old windows. Meanwhile, the house stands in its shady corner above the mill race, its lovely soft stone dappled in the sunlight, a testament to the workmanship of the families who came here so long ago.

One of the most dramatic buildings outside the stone fiefdom of Finesville is the Cline barn, an arched, three-story, limestone barn of rare and original construction in the countryside near Springtown. Owner Stephen Babinsky says it is Germanic in nature (not surprisingly, given the region's heavy German immigrant population), but it displays English construction techniques, dating from around 1800 to 1810. The Cline family bought the barn after it was built and gave it its name.

The south-facing wall has four arches offering entry to the ground floor. The portals of the arches are beautifully picked out in brick. Matching arches decorate the north façade, which opens into a third-floor hayloft, reached by a bridge. Nearly all the timbers in the barn, including the roof rafters, are hand-hewn white oak. "The flooring was originally two-inch-thick white oak planks and was not nailed but actually held down with wooden pegs or 'tree nails,'" explains Steve Babinsky. He also points to the unusual louvered ventilators in the exterior walls. A pedimented window opening from the hayloft is another sophisticated detail.

The barn is part of a complex of buildings on the property, including an eighteenth-century stone house, wagon sheds, corncribs, and a mill built in 1786. Steve Babinsky refers to the estate as "an eighteenth-century industrial park." (He also owns another circa-1800 stone house in Finesville, known as the Fabian & Seyler House, opposite Fine's Wool Manufactory, which is full of eighteenth- and nineteenth-century museum-quality furniture.) The barn is now home to horses, but its elegant architecture could well accommodate a much grander clientele. Almost Italianate, yet with that solid look of colonial eighteenth-century confidence, the Cline barn is perhaps the most striking example of the region's vernacular style.

The graceful arcade is decorated with brick portals, an extraordinarily sophisticated addition to the façade of what is simply a farm building.

This stunningly elegant three-story limestone barn, with four arches at ground level and a pedimented window opening at the center of the building, was built in approximately 1800 and shortly afterwards purchased by the Cline family.

RIGHT *The interior of the Cline barn is as interesting as the exterior, with ceiling timbers of white oak and a series of louvered windows to allow light and ventilation.*

BELOW LEFT *The south side of the barn, showing the access at the third-floor level.*

BELOW CENTER *The main farmhouse, also built of the same limestone, with handsome Georgian-style fifteen-pane windows original to the house.*

BELOW RIGHT *A little urban archeology adds atmosphere to this stylish farm complex.*

BENJAMIN SEIGLE HOUSE

Unlike the collection of stone houses in Finesville, the Benjamin Seigle House is made of different materials. This house is the only surviving two-story log homestead of its type in Warren County. It was built in approximately 1793 on land owned by Benjamin Seigle, who came to New Jersey from Bucks County, Pennsylvania, to farm—and probably to start the pottery that his son, Jacob, turned into such a success.

Just as the ancient Greeks created their columns by building them stone by stone, in strict order, so the builders of the Seigle House created the walls of the building by laying logs on top of each other so skillfully that while most wooden structures rot or disintegrate over time, this homestead still braves the elements almost unimpaired after more than two hundred

The eighteenth-century garden was added by the present owners. Its formal design, reminiscent of the gardens in Colonial Williamsburg, harmonizes beautifully with the style of the house.

years. The wood used is walnut, a hardwood, roughly one foot square, cut down during the summertime when the wood is at its strongest. The logs are held together—in a method called "chinking"—by a mixture of limestone and mortar. The effect of the horizontal stripes created by the chinking is as decorative as a tapestry.

The house is two stories high, but the levels are confusing since it is built against the side of a hill; thus the cellar is at ground level, and the entrance is up a flight of steps. Much of the window glass is original, as is the interior stairway. Marks of hinges in the wall indicate that the house originally had shutters. The front door has a latch, custom-made in the style of the period, for the current owners, Jeffrey and Kim Finegan. There is a central chimney in the inner ground-floor entrance hall that the owners believe may have been built before the walls were constructed. On the second floor, the fireplace is set at an angle in a corner of the room, a not uncommon design feature of the period, allowing the heat to circulate more efficiently.

The Finegans, who bought the house fourteen years ago, have restored it with great care. In 1992, needing more space for their family, they added a section to the north side of the house, using period construction materials and creating a simulated whitewash finish for the exterior that would not offend the earlier structure. They chose random cypress floorboards, small square window panes, and other colonial detailing, all of which make the addition feel perfectly at home with its older neighbor. They also designed a lovely little eighteenth-century garden at the back of the house, overlooked by a spectacular dovecote, inspired by one Jeff Finegan saw in Colonial Williamsburg.

ABOVE *The house is built of walnut logs, laid on top of each other, with chinking made of limestone and mortar. This visually striking combination of materials turned out to be so sturdy that it allowed the structure to survive far longer than most wooden houses of the period.*
FACING *The log homestead was built in approximately 1793. The whitewashed addition, only ten years old, was designed with copies of eighteenth- and nineteenth-century materials by the present owners. The splendid fence is of the period.*

ABOVE *In the back hall, as in the rest of the house, there are many original features, including floorboards and a large cooking hearth, ornamented with a wood mantel.* FACING TOP LEFT *Beds of clipped ivy and carefully placed containers decorate the back terrace. The old door opens into the back hall and living room.* FACING TOP RIGHT *The dovecote, like the garden, was inspired by one in Colonial Williamsburg.* FACING BOTTOM *This woolly creature, like the rest of the property, dates back to the eighteenth century. George Washington is said to have owned a similar flock at Mount Vernon.*

On the hillside to the north graze some rather unusual-looking sheep. Could they also date from the eighteenth century? "Of course," Jeff Finegan declares. "George Washington is said to have owned a similar flock at Mount Vernon. They are called Hog Island sheep, favorites of northern Virginia planters in the eighteenth century." In Benjamin Seigle's will, probated in 1798, he provided for his widow to receive, among other household property, two cows, a riding horse, and three sheep. Jeff Finegan feels confident that he will be able to make the same provisions for his wife—at least with regard to the sheep.

This little corner of New Jersey evokes the eighteenth-century world of farmers, mill owners, and craftsmen living off the land, and the Benjamin Seigle House epitomizes the period most authentically. (It is now on the National Register of Historic Places.) Its charm, well-wrought construction, and surroundings, like those of the classic stone houses of Finesville, speak so vividly of their time that we are irresistibly drawn back to the country's simpler past.

BIBLIOGRAPHY

Abrams, Janet, et al. *Michael Graves: Buildings and Projects, 1990–1994*. New York: Rizzoli, 1995.

Arcadia Publishing has produced books with black-and-white archival photographs and postcards on the history of over 150 New Jersey townships in their "Images of America" series. Dover, N.H.: Arcadia Publishing.

Bisgrove, Richard. *The Gardens of Gertrude Jekyll*. Photography by Andrew Lawson. Berkeley: University of California Press, 2000.

Brady, Joan B. *Another Kind of Time*. Amityville, N.Y.: aah-ha! Books, Inc., 1999.

Brown, T. Robins, and Schuyler Warmflash. *The Architecture of Bergen County, New Jersey, The Colonial Period to the Twentieth Century*. New Brunswick, N.J.: Rutgers University Press, 2001.

Cathers, David M. *Stickley Style: Arts and Crafts Homes in the Craftsman Tradition*. Photography by Alexander Vertikoff. New York: Simon & Schuster, 1999.

Gowans, Alan. *Architecture in New Jersey*. New York: Van Nostrand Co., 1964.

Graves, Michael. *Michael Graves: Selected and Current Works*. Edited by Stephen Dobney. New York: Images, 1999.

Hand, Susanne C. *New Jersey Architecture*. Trenton, N.J.: New Jersey Historical Commission, 1995.

Hewitt, Mark Alan. *The Architect & the American Country House, 1890–1940*. New Haven, Conn.: Yale University Press, 1990.

Hobhouse, Penelope. *The Country Gardener*. New York: Frances Lincoln, Ltd., 2000.

Hobhouse, Penelope. *Penelope Hobhouse on Gardening*. New York: Frances Lincoln, Ltd., 2000.

Hobhouse, Penelope, and Simon Johnson. *Penelope Hobhouse's Garden Designs*. New York: Henry Holt & Co., 1997.

Jekyll, Gertrude. *Color Schemes for the Flower Garden*. New York: Frances Lincoln, Ltd., 2001.

Jekyll, Gertrude, and Lawrence Weaver. *Gardens for Small Country Houses*. New York: C. Scribner's Sons, 1913.

Lacy, Allen. *A Year in Our Gardens: Letters of Nancy Goodwin and Allen Lacy*. Chapel Hill: University of North Carolina Press, 2001.

Love, Paul. *Patterned Brickwork in Southern New Jersey*. Proceedings of the New Jersey Historical Society, 1955.

McAdoo, Eleanor Wilson, in collaboration with Margaret Y. Gaffey. *The Woodrow Wilsons*. New York: Macmillan, 1937.

Meier, Richard. *Richard Meier Houses*. Introduction by Paul Goldberger. New York: Rizzoli International Publishers, 1996.

Meier, Richard, Joseph Rykwert, and Kenneth Frampton. *Richard Meier, Architect: 1992/1999, Volume 3*. New York: Rizzoli International Publications, 1999.

Mellick, Andrew D., Jr.. *The Old Farm*. New Brunswick, N.J.: Rutgers University Press, 1961.

Salvini, Emil R. *The Summer City by the Sea: Cape May, New Jersey—An Illustrated History*. New Brunswick, N.J.: Rutgers University Press, 1995.

Schwartz, Helen. *The New Jersey House*. Photographs by Margaret Morgan Fisher. New Brunswick, N.J.: Rutgers University Press, 1990.

Seebohm, Caroline. *Boca Rococo: How Addison Mizner Invented Florida's Gold Coast*. New York: Clarkson Potter, 2001.

Snell, James P. *History of Hunterdon and Somerset Counties, New Jersey, Volume II*. Philadelphia, Pa.: Everts & Peck, 1881.

Stickley, Gustav. *Craftsman Homes: Architecture and Furnishings of the American Arts and Crafts Movement*. 1909. Reprint, New York: Dover Publications, 1979.

Thomas, George E. *Cape May, Queen of the Seaside Resorts: Its History and Architecture*. Philadelphia, Pa.: Associated University Presses, 1998.

Venturi, Robert. *Complexity and Contradiction in Architecture*. New York: Museum of Modern Art, 2002.

Venturi, Robert, Steven Izenour, and Denise Scott Brown. *Learning from Las Vegas*. Cambridge, Mass.: M.I.T. Press, 1972.

Wright, Frank Lloyd. *In the Cause of Architecture: Wright's Historic Essays for Architectural Record, 1908–1952*. An *Architectural Record* Book. New York: McGraw Hill, 1975.

Zion, Robert L. *Trees for Architecture and Landscape*. New York: Van Nostrand Reinhold, 1995.

INDEX

ABOUT THE AUTHOR AND PHOTOGRAPHER

CAROLINE SEEBOHM was born and grew up in England. She was on the staff of
House & Garden magazine in New York for seven years before becoming a freelance writer.
She has published several books on architecture and design, including *Boca Rococo:
How Addison Mizner Invented Florida's Gold Coast* and *Under Live Oaks: The Last
Great Houses of the Old South*. She lives on the Delaware River in Titusville, New Jersey.

PETER C. COOK studied photography at The School of Visual Arts and has been
working professionally for twenty-three years. He lives in Lambertville, New Jersey.

*Produced by Wilsted & Taylor Publishing Services:
Copyediting by Caroline Roberts
Design and composition by Jeff Clark*